CRITICAL ACCLAIM FOR THE WORKS OF JAMES RADA, JR.

I0569826

The Last to Fall

"Authors Jim Rada and Richard Fulton have done an outstanding job of researching and chronicling this little-known story of those Marines in 1922, marking it as a significant moment in Marine Corps history."

- *GySgt. Thomas Williams*
Executive Director
U.S. Marine Corps Historical Company

"Original, unique, profusely illustrated throughout, exceptionally well researched, informed, informative, and a bit iconoclastic, "The Last to Fall: The 1922 March, Battles, & Deaths of U.S. Marines at Gettysburg" will prove to be of enormous interest to military buffs and historians."

- *Small Press Bookwatch*

Saving Shallmar

"But Saving Shallmar's Christmas story is a tale of compassion and charity, and the will to help fellow human beings not only survive, but also be ready to spring into action when a new opportunity presents itself. Bittersweet yet heartwarming, Saving Shallmar is a wonderful Christmas season story for readers of all ages and backgrounds, highly recommended."

- *Small Press Bookwatch*

Battlefield Angels

"Rada describes women religious who selflessly performed life-saving work in often miserable conditions and thereby gained the admiration and respect of countless contemporaries. In so doing, Rada offers an appealing narrative and an entry point into the wealth of sources kept by the sisters."

- *Catholic News Service*

Between Rail and River

"The book is an enjoyable, clean family read, with characters young and old for a broad-based appeal to both teens and adults. Between Rail and River also provides a unique, regional appeal, as it teaches about a particular group of people, ordinary working 'canawlers' in a story that goes beyond the usual coverage of life during the Civil War."

- *Historical Fiction Review*

Canawlers

"A powerful, thoughtful and fascinating historical novel, Canawlers documents author James Rada, Jr. as a writer of considerable and deftly expressed storytelling talent."

- *Midwest Book Review*

"James Rada, of Cumberland, has written a historical novel for high-schoolers and adults, which relates the adventures, hardships and ultimate tragedy of a family of boaters on the C&O Canal. ... The tale moves quickly and should hold the attention of readers looking for an imaginative adventure set on the canal at a critical time in history."

- *Along the Towpath*

October Mourning

"This is a very good, and very easy to read, novel about a famous, yet unknown, bit of 20th Century American history. While reading this book, in your mind, replace all mentions of 'Spanish Flu' with 'bird flu.' Hmmm."

- *Reviewer's Bookwatch*

Continue your adventure in history with three FREE historical novels from James Rada, Jr.

Visit *jamesrada.com / newsletter-email*
and enter your email
to receive your FREE novels.

SECRETS OF
DEEP CREEK LAKE

Little-Known Stories & Hidden History In
and Around Maryland's Largest Lake

Other books by James Rada, Jr.

Non-Fiction

- Battlefield Angels: The Daughters of Charity Work as Civil War Nurses
- Beyond the Battlefield: Stories from Gettysburg's Rich History
- Clay Soldiers: One Marine's Story of War, Art, & Atomic Energy
- Echoes of War Drums: The Civil War in Mountain Maryland
- How to Make a Living Freelance Writing
- The Last to Fall: The 1922 March, Battles & Deaths of U.S. Marines at Gettysburg
- Looking Back: True Stories of Mountain Maryland
- Looking Back II: More True Stories of Mountain Maryland
- No North, No South: The Grand Reunion at the 50th Anniversary of the Battle of Gettysburg
- Saving Shallmar: Christmas Spirit in a Coal Town

Black Fire Trilogy

- Smoldering Betrayal
- Strike the Fuse
- Frostburg Burning

Secrets Series

- Secrets of Allegany County: Little-Known Stories & Hidden History From Mountain Maryland
- Secrets of Catoctin Mountain: Little-Known Stories & Hidden History Along Catoctin Mountain
- Secrets of Franklin County: Little-Known Stories & Hidden History on Pennsylvania's State Line
- Secrets of Garrett County: Little-Known Stories & Hidden History of Maryland's Westernmost County
- Secrets of the C&O Canal: Little-Known Stories & Hidden History Along the Potomac River
- Secrets of the Gettysburg Battlefield: Little-Known Stories & Hidden History from the Gettysburg Battlefield
- Secrets of the Washington County: Little-Known Stories & Hidden History Where Western Maryland Starts

Canawlers Series

- Between Rail and River
- Canawlers
- Lock Ready

Fiction

- October Mourning
- The Rain Man

SECRETS OF
DEEP CREEK LAKE

Little-Known Stories & Hidden History In
and Around Maryland's Largest Lake

by
James Rada, Jr.

LEGACY
PUBLISHING
A division of AIM Publishing Group

SECRETS OF DEEP CREEK LAKE: LITTLE-KNOWN STORIES
AND HIDDEN HISTORY IN AND AROUND MARYLAND'S
LARGEST LAKE

Published by Legacy Publishing, a division of AIM Publishing Group.
Gettysburg, Pennsylvania.
Printed in the United States of America.
First printing: April 2023.

ISBN 978-1-7352890-9-0

This is a collection primarily of articles that have previously appeared in
The Cumberland Times-News and *The Republican* newspapers. In some
cases where additional information is available the stories have been updated.

Cover design by Grace Eyler.

LEGACY
PUBLISHING
315 Oak Lane • Gettysburg, Pennsylvania 17325

CONTENTS

Deep Creek Lake

P eople in Garrett County today can't remember a time when the county didn't have Deep Creek Lake, although there was one. As Deep Creek Lakes turns 100 years old (in 2025), most people consider it a magnificent tourist attraction in Garrett County and the largest freshwater lake in Maryland. Both are true, but Deep Creek Lake didn't start out that way.

The idea of using hydroelectric power for the county was first posed in 1908. Financing couldn't be secured, so the idea was dropped.

When it was revived, the power generation wasn't planned for use in Garrett County, but for Pennsylvania. The Youghiogheny Hydroelectric Company project started in the 1922. Besides purchasing farms and properties in the McHenry area, a hydroelectric plant and earth and rock wall dam needed to be built. The dam is built across Deep Creek, a tributary of the Youghiogheny River.

The project employed 1,000 men. They built the dam and power plant. They cleared the trees and other objects from the valley where the water would be held.

Groundbreaking for the dam happened on November 1, 1923. Once it was built, streams and rivers in the area had their flows blocked and the valley filled over several months. The major stream that was blocked, and the one that gives the lake its name, was Deep Creek. However, Deep Creek, which is between Roman Nose Ridge and Marsh Hill Ridge, is fed by other streams, namely North Glade, Meadow Mountain, and Cherry Run.

Besides the dam, steel bridges had to be built to carry vehicles over the new lake and roads that would soon be underwater had to be re-routed.

The project, which employed 1,000 men, also required a lot of infrastructure to support it. A rail connection to Oakland was built to transport heavy equipment and material to the construction site. A quarry to provide the stone needed for the construction was opened.

The hydroelectric plant went operational at 4 p.m. on May 26, 1925, and still operates today. The area around the lake remained sparsely populated, hindered by the Great Depression and then World War II. However, when the area's economy grew quickly after the war, so did the Deep Creek Lake area.

The State of Maryland purchased the land beneath the lake in 2000 from the Pennsylvania Electric Company, and the Maryland Department of Natural Resources manages it. The dam is now used to control water flows to maintain the river temperature and dissolved oxygen levels to help downstream fisheries increase the number of trout. The dam control releases are also benefit whitewater activities on the Upper Youghiogheny River.

The lake continues to be a popular destination for fishing, boating, and water skiing. In the winter, if the lake freezes over, you will also see people ice fishing on the lake.

Today, the lake covers 3,900 acres with sixty-five miles of shoreline. It averages twenty-six feet in depth with some areas being seventy-five-feet deep.

Besides creating tourism jobs in the area, the lake generates the bulk of the county's real estate tax income. This is because the lake made property in the area more valuable, particularly home lots along the shoreline.

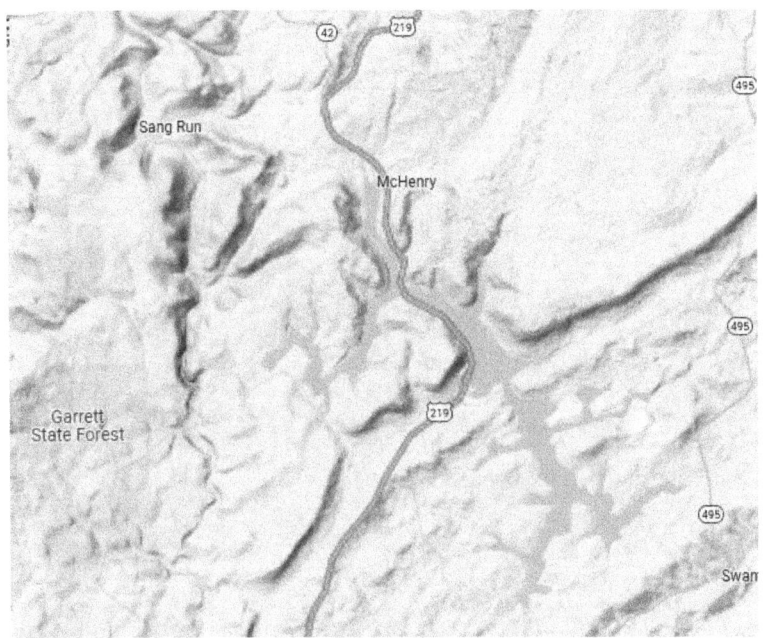

Deep Creek Lake. Courtesy of Mapquest.com.

Quick Facts

- Garrett County Population: about 31,000.
- Annual Visitors: about 1.4 million (although all aren't visiting the lake, the majority are).
- Annual Visitor Spending: $314 million.
- Annual Tourism Economic Impact: $360 million.
- Cost of Land Purchased for Lake: $5 to $2,500 an acre (average $55).
- Acres Purchased: Almost 8,000 (only 4,500 acres were flooded).
- Farms Purchased: 140.
- Buildings Purchased or Moved: 52.

Source: Visitdeepcreek.com and Garrett County.

INTERESTING PEOPLE

Big Mac's Creator Loved Deep Creek Lake

C ustomers of the Uniontown, Pennsylvania, McDonald's pondered a new menu item in April 1967. For 45 cents, they could get "two all-beef patties, special sauce, lettuce, cheese, pickles, onions, on a sesame-seed bun." Just a few years later, this recipe would be something just about any American could sing, but in 1967, the Big Mac was something new and different.

And people loved it. The *New York Times* wrote, "A year later, the Big Mac was on the menu at McDonald's restaurants all over the United States. By 1969, it accounted for 19 percent of the company's total sales. Today, the company sells about 550 million Big Macs annually in the United States alone, and millions more in 100 countries around the world."

Jim Delligatti created this piece of Americana. He is generally associated with the Pittsburgh area. That is where he lived in Fox Chapel and where his first McDonald's franchises were located, but he also played a part in the development of the Deep Creek Lake area.

Delligatti opened his first McDonald's in 1957, and about a decade later, he owned a dozen restaurants. Back then, his major competition came from the Big Boy and Burger King chains.

Looking for a way to overcome the competition, Delligatti "proposed to company executives that they add a double-patty hamburger to the McDonald's menu, something along the lines of the Big Boy, that could put a dent in sales of Burger King's Whopper," according to the *New York Times*.

At the time, McDonald's had a limited menu that focused on the basics, such as a hamburger that cost eighteen cents. McDonald's executives worried that a higher-priced burger wouldn't be accepted by their customers.

Jim Delligatti holds up two of his creations, the iconic McDonald's Big Mac sandwiches. Photo courtesy of Instagram.com.

Ralph Lanphar, a regional manager in Columbus, Ohio, headquarters shared Delligatti's vision and got permission for Delligatti to test the Big Mac in Uniontown, using only McDonald's ingredients.

This didn't work, though, because the ingredients didn't fit the McDonald's bun "so Mr. Delligatti went rogue, ordering a large sesame-seeded bun from a local baker. He split it in three and assembled the Big Mac as the world knows it today, with a special sauce of his own devising," according to the *New York Times.*

The Big Mac debuted on April 22, 1967, and was an immediate hit as seen by the increase in sales.

"At one time we were the lowest-volume store of any large city," Delligatti said in a 1993 *Los Angeles Times* interview. "A few years after the Big Mac introduction, we became the largest — a distinction we held for a couple of years."

Delligatti was allowed to introduce the Big Mac to his other restaurants, which saw similar jumps in sales. It was then rolled out across the country.

Although Delligatti eventually owned forty-eight McDonald's restaurants, his impact in Garrett County was felt in a different way.

However, he also had strong ties with the Deep Creek Lake area. The Delligattis not only owned a vacation home on Deep Creek Lake, they helped develop the area.

Delligatti owned or was a business partner in Uno's Pizza, Arrowhead Condominiums, The Honi Honi Bar, Garrett 8 Cinemas, and Arrowhead Market in McHenry. All of which continue to draw customers and tourists year round.

"We've been coming here for 35 years," Delligatti told the *Cumberland Times-News* in 1994. "We love Garrett County. My wife remembers the old Blue Barn and we wanted to do something to help the county."

Besides inventing the Big Mac, Delligatti also developed the Hotcakes and Sausage meal to feed hungry steel workers on their way home from overnight shifts in the mills.

In 1979, he co-founded Pittsburgh's Ronald McDonald House, a refuge for families who travel to Pittsburgh seeking life-saving medical care for their sick children at the region's renowned hospitals. He was also a strong supporter of Children's Hospital of Pittsburgh, Junior Achievement of Southwestern PA, the Cystic Fibrosis Foundation, Boy Scouts of America, and the Leukemia & Lymphoma Society.

Delligatti died at his home in Fox Chapel in 2016 at ninety-eight.

The Vagabonds' Camping Trip Near Deep Creek Lake

S ometimes you just need to get away from work. It doesn't matter if you are a leader of industry or someone who works for such a leader. In 1914, Henry Ford, Thomas Edison, Harvey Firestone, and John Burroughs discovered they got along well together and enjoyed each other's company. They started making plans for summer vacations where they would travel around the country in cars Ford's company built by Ford on tires Firestone's company manufactured.

They called themselves the Vagabonds.

Over the years their meeting, they got together to travel along the East Coast and into the Midwest. Their stops included New England, West Virginia, North Carolina, Michigan, Tennessee, Virginia, Massachusetts, and Maryland. They seemed to favor mountain settings like the Appalachians, Catskills and Adirondacks.

Although the Vagabonds camped out during these road trips, they weren't roughing it on these trips by any stretch of the imagination.

According to The Henry Ford Foundation, "The 1919 trip involved fifty vehicles, including two designed by Ford: a kitchen camping car with a gasoline stove and built-in icebox presided over by a cook and a heavy touring car mounted on a truck chassis with compartments for tents, cots, chairs, electric lights, etc. On later trips, there was a huge, folding round table equipped with a lazy susan that seated twenty."

Household staff traveled with the men to cook, clean, and pack for them. Ford Motor Company photographers also accompanied the group to document the events.

Nowadays, this would be called glamping, which is camping, but with the luxuries of home.

One of the Vagabonds' early trips passed through Garrett County with a mid-day stop near Oakland to rest and eat. Their itinerary for the day started on Summit Mountain in Pennsylvania. They made a quick stop in Keyser's Ridge to pick up mail and then headed south through Garrett County, passing through Oakland on their way to Horse Shoe Run, where they made camp for the night.

During an early vacation, the Vagabonds passed through Garrett County and took a noon rest break near Oakland. Harvey Firestone is reading the newspaper on the left and John Burroughs is lying on his side. Photo courtesy of the Library of Congress.

In 1921, however, changes happened with the Vagabonds' trip. The first change was that the four vagabonds became three with the death of naturalist and writer John Burroughs on March 29, 1921. Firestone, Ford, and Edison decided they would still vacation, but they would find a way to honor their friend.

They decided to include an honorary Vagabond, not to replace Burroughs, but simply to have another notable person camping with them. This honorary Vagabond turned out to be President Warren G. Harding.

Firestone and his friend, Bishop William F. Anderson of Ohio, visited President Harding at the White House and invited him to join the camping trip in late July. Harding and Firestone were longtime friends. The President accepted, but he needed the camping trip to travel within a reasonable driving distance of Washington, D.C. in case he might be needed in the capital city quickly.

"Unfortunately, during the week of July 17, Mrs. Harding became ill, and the President had to delay his rendezvous with the campers for several days, until he was certain his wife was in no danger," the *Model T Times* reported.

Harding wouldn't be able to accompany the Vagabonds on the entire trip, but he would camp with them on July 23, 1921, near Licking Creek in Maryland. The area is now called Camp Harding County Park in Washington County, Maryland, and a plaque there commemorates the location of the campsite.

Another change was that the men included their wives on the trip, something to which Edison objected. "Edison was concerned that the wives would not 'appreciate the primitiveness of camp conditions or take pleasure in roaming over the unbeaten track,'" according to *Model T Times*.

The change that was most important to Western Maryland is that instead of traveling all day and camping for a single night at each stop, they decided to actually enjoy the camping as well as the traveling. They extended their stay at two Western Maryland campsites before traveling into West

Virginia.

From July 22 to July 27, the Vagabonds camped on Licking Creek near Pecktonville in Washington County. Following this stop, they camped from July 27 to July 31 near Muddy Creek Falls in McHenry.

On July 21, Ford and his wife, Clara, sailed from Detroit,
Michigan, to Cleveland, Ohio, along Lake Erie on their
yacht. They met Firestone in Akron, Ohio, and traveled to the
Firestone homestead in Columbiana, Ohio, to meet up with
Harvey Firestone, Jr. and his new bride, along with Fire-
stone's other son, Russel.

The Fords' son, Edsel, and his wife also visited the
homestead. The Women's Missionary Society of the Grace
Reformed Church served the group dinner. From there, they
drove to Bedford Springs and spent the night. The next day,
the Fords and Firestones drove to Hagerstown where they
met the Edisons, who had arrived from West Orange, New
Jersey, and Anderson and his wife, who arrived from Washington, D.C.

They ate lunch there, and then the group went to Pecktonville, near Big Pool. They set up camp along Licking
Creek on a 200-acre farm. "The camp was quite elaborate
with numerous tents and nearly fifty cots for sleeping," the
Model T Times reported. "A special electric lighting system
was erected and even a large truckload of food from the Firestone farm arrived, which contained two refrigerators with
several hundred pounds of meat, butter, eggs, milk, melons,
and one hundred dressed chickens. All the meals were prepared by Chefs Fisher and Herman. There was also a special
padded truck which brought six of Firestone's finest riding
horses all the way from Akron."

Edison thought all the preparations were too extravagant.
He liked his camping to be more rustic. "Ford and Firestone

quickly reminded him that he had contributed to the setup with his special electrical lighting equipment and a portable radio, which was a rare item in those days," the *Model T Times* reported.

After the evening campfire conversations, the entire group retired early to get a good night's sleep to prepare for the arrival of President Harding the next day.

President Harding becomes a Vagabond

Henry Ford, Thomas Edison, Harvey Firestone, and John Burroughs were friends who enjoyed traveling and camping together in the early 1900s. They called themselves the Vagabonds. However, in 1921, Burroughs died, leaving an empty spot among the group.

Firestone and President Warren G. Harding were long-time friends. Firestone invited the President to join the Vagabonds on their trip. Harding accepted, but he wasn't able to accompany them on their entire trip. Instead, he said he could join them on July 23 at their campsite near Licking Creek. The area in Washington County is now called Camp Harding County Park.

"Selection of Harding to take the vacant place in this camping club of distinguished men is considered one of the most unique honors conferred since he became President," the *Frederick News* reported.

The President left Washington, D.C. at 9:30 a.m. He must have been eager to get away overnight because he averaged fifty miles per hour on the trip there.

"The Secret Service and the many journalists and photographers had difficulty keeping up with the President's car as it journeyed toward Funkstown," according to The *Model T Times*. "He arrived shortly after Ford, Firestone, Edison, and company arrived."

They arrived at the campsite on Licking Creek around 1 p.m. The group ate lunch in a dining tent with at a table that had a lazy Susan that had a nine-foot diameter.

After lunch, the men enjoyed a casual afternoon. The President took a nap in his tent. Ford and Firestone competed in a wood-chopping contest. Edison laid down under an elm tree and took a nap.

When Harding woke up, he, Ford, and Firestone went horseback riding. Harding's personal secretary, George Christian, and Secret Service agent, Colonel Edmund Starling, accompanied them.

"The President then visited a local general store and made a phone call back to the White House to check on the health of his wife," the *Model T Times* reported. "While there, he bought candy for several local children gathered at the store."

Back at camp, the group enjoyed a hearty dinner. Music was provided by a player piano powered by a portable electric generator. The Vagabonds stayed up to 2 a.m., talking and telling stories around a campfire.

The following day, the group went horseback riding after breakfast.

After the ride, Bishop Anderson held a Sunday morning worship and memorial service in memory of Burroughs, one of the original Vagabonds.

"Mrs. Firestone played the piano and the congregation sang hymns," the *Model T Times* reported. "There were several hundred in attendance, as many local farmers and visitors joined the service. The service concluded with the audience joining President Harding in singing 'Rock of Ages' and 'Nearer My God to Thee'."

They lunched at the campsite, and Harding and his entourage left around 4 p.m. to return to Washington. It had been a quick getaway for Harding, but the trip was only beginning for the remaining Vagabonds.

Thomas Edison enjoys an outdoor nap while Harvey Firestone and President Warren Harding sit and relax. Courtesy of the Library of Congress.

The Vagabonds in Garrett County

Henry Ford, Thomas Edison, Harvey Firestone, and John Burroughs were friends who called themselves the Vagabonds. They enjoyed traveling and camping together in the early 1900s until Burroughs died in 1921. President Warren G. Harding took Burroughs' place for one night during the Vagabonds' 1921 camping trip, but he couldn't continue with the group as they traveled west from Washington County into Allegany County.

Harding spent July 23 with the group, and then headed back to Washington, D.C. late afternoon of the next day. On July 25, the remaining Vagabonds began planning their next destination while still enjoying the campground along Licking Creek in Washington County.

On July 27, they broke camp, made their way to the National Road, and headed west toward Garrett County. They stopped for lunch in a field near Deer Park and then moved on to the Swallow Falls area.

"It is said that Fred W. Besley, Maryland's first forester, recommended Swallow Falls for the campsite. A fortunate choice it was, too. This is probably the most scenic region of Maryland," Caleb Winslow wrote in *Journal of the Alleghenies*.

The campsite was an area filled with virgin hemlock and fir trees, but to get to it, they had to cross a small wooden bridge.

"The first cars made it across, but the bridge collapsed under the weight of the heavy camp kitchen truck and blocked the path of the remaining vehicles carrying the supplies," the *Model T Times* reported.

Members of the group had to carry the supplies to an open clearing near Muddy Creek, the highest natural waterfall in Maryland. It was a perfect campsite.

Unfortunately, they weren't the only ones to think so. They found a group of young boys from Oakland had already camped there.

According to Joseph Hinebaugh, who was a boy in the group, Ford paid the boys to move to a different campsite. "The boys visited the famous campers several times and eagerly accepted candy and other treats," according to the *Model T Times*. "They had the opportunity to inspect the method the ingenious Edison used to illuminate the camp by obtaining electrical current from the batteries of the automobiles for the light bulbs strung around the tents."

After a long day of travel and a lot of physical work hauling supplies, the Vagabonds and their entourage went to bed early and slept late the next morning.

They relaxed on July 28, and the broken bridge kept visitors away from the area who might want to see the famous trio. This gave the men some relative seclusion. The men swam in the creek and around the waterfalls. They hiked trails in the area. Edison, in particular, enjoyed sitting by the falls and relaxing.

"Ford enjoyed hiking the back roads looking for anything old or mechanical," the *Model T Times* reported. "He discovered an old steam engine at a nearby sawmill and wanted to purchase it."

Newton Reams, who owned the steam engine, visited Ford at the camp. According to Reams, Ford reached into his pocket and paid for the engine with two $50 bills. Ford examined the engine and asked Reams if he could find a missing part.

Reams went to a neighbor who had a similar engine and asked to buy the part. The neighbor would only sell the entire engine, and he wanted $75. Reams told Ford he would need to buy an entire second engine to get the missing part.

"How much?" Ford asked.

Reams doubled the price. Ford again reached into his pocket and pulled out three $50 bills. Reams took both engines to Oakland and shipped them by train to Dearborn, Michigan, while pocketing a nice profit for his work.

During their stay, Ford's Lincoln automobile got stuck in the mud, and a resident hooked his horses to the car to pull it out.

A young boy, not knowing who Ford was, allegedly said, "Mister, you have the wrong kind of car. My father drives a Ford, and it never gets stuck on this road."

Ford delighted in the testimonial. He wrote the name and address of the boy's father, and when he returned home, sent the man a brand new Model T.

Henry Sines and his brother, Abraham Lincoln "Link" Sines, spent time at the Vagabonds' camp. The brothers shared stories about the area with the group. Link was a forest warden and master woodsman. He had met the Vagabonds, including John Burroughs, in 1918, when they passed through Garrett County. Now with Burroughs gone, Link served as a guide and naturalist for the Vagabonds.

Link later wrote about how the Vagabonds spent their time. "Ford loved anything mechanical. He was constantly looking for items to add to his collection in Detroit. Firestone liked to fish. Edison was either reading a book or tinkering with his Packard. Burroughs knew more about trees and plants than anyone I ever met."

Once, R. Emerson Cross and his friends rented horses in Oakland and rode into the Vagabonds' camp while they were riding in the Muddy Creek area. The Vagabonds asked if they could borrow the horses to ride. Cross agreed, and when the Vagabonds returned from their ride, they gave Cross and his friends $30. Cross was delighted, since they only paid $1.25 each to rent the horses.

Harvey Firestone and Henry Ford get lunch at one of the Vagabonds' campsites. Photo courtesy of the Library of Congress.

Leaving a legacy behind

In 1921, Henry Ford, Thomas Edison, Harvey Firestone, and their entourage camped near Swallow Falls in July. The men had been taking summer camping and driving trips since 1918, though this was the first year they had done it without the fourth "Vagabond," John Burroughs. Despite an early mishap with a collapsed bridge on their way to the campsite, the men enjoyed their time in Garrett County, hiking and swimming. As their time in the county came to an end, they had to decide where to venture next. It was decided they would visit the Cheat River in West Virginia.

However, on July 30, when they were scheduled to break camp, a severe rainstorm hit the area and soaked the area for hours. The road leading out of the campsite became impassable because of mud, and the group had to remain another day. This gave the ground time to dry out somewhat so their vehicles wouldn't get stuck in the mud as they made their way back to the road. Even with the delay, some of the vehicles had problems. A big truck that carried the camping equipment got stuck and had to be pulled out by a tractor while the other vehicles continued.

The group spent the night of July 31 in Elkins, but since the truck with the camping gear hadn't arrived, they spent the night in a hotel instead of tents. They made it to the Cheat River the next day, but then had to start their journey home because of both Ford's and Firestone's offices had been trying to find out when they would return to deal with business issues.

The return journey went through Fairmont, Morgantown, and Uniontown, where they stayed at the Summit Inn. That evening at the Summit Hotel, Edison showed off his agility by kicking a cigar off the mantle in the hotel lobby three times in a row. He and Ford competed in a "stair jumping" contest on the lobby stairs. Ford jumped up ten steps in two hops. Edison needed three hops to jump the same ten stairs.

From Uniontown, the group went to Pittsburgh, where the Vagabonds went their separate ways to return home.

The Vagabonds' camping trips continued until 1924. At that point, the men were too well known to go camping and enjoy their leisure time, undisturbed by the public.

In 2018, a special tour was held to commemorate the centennial anniversary of the first August 1918 Vagabonds camping trip, which also included a stop in Garrett County for lunch. The tour began at the Summit Inn near Uniontown and retraced the Vagabonds' trip on the same dates as the original trip.

Today, a Maryland Historical Society Marker in Swallow Falls State Park shows where the Vagabonds made camp while in Garrett County.

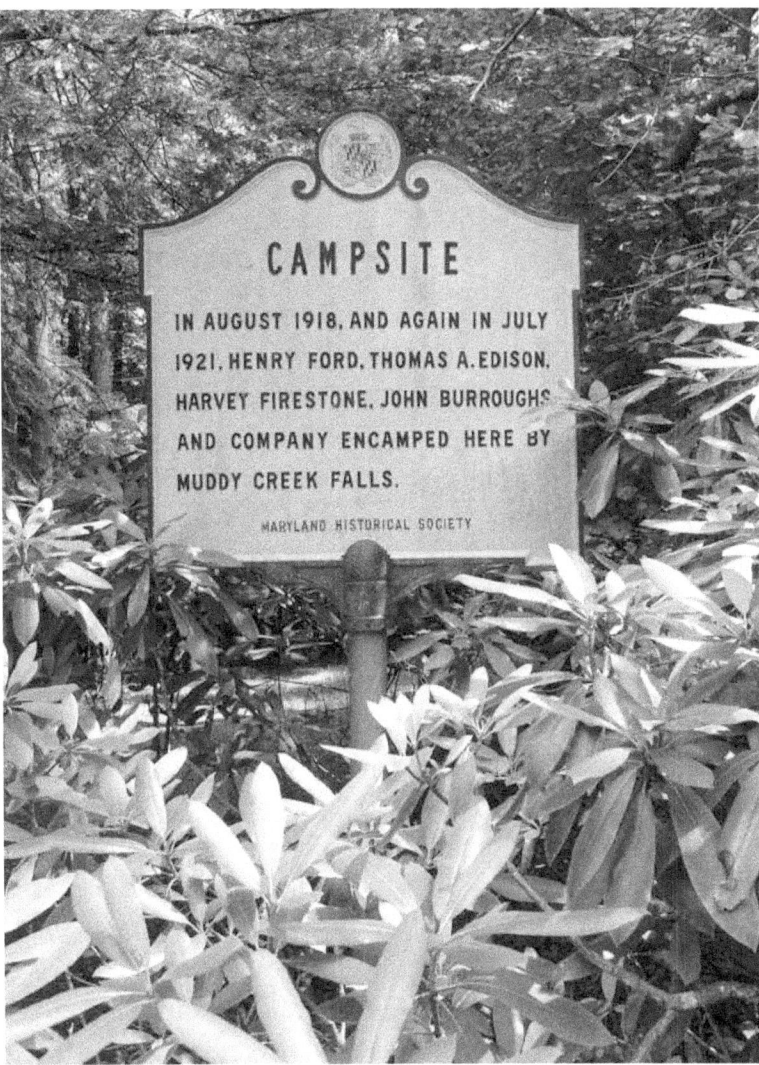

CAMPSITE

IN AUGUST 1918, AND AGAIN IN JULY
1921, HENRY FORD, THOMAS A. EDISON,
HARVEY FIRESTONE, JOHN BURROUGHS
AND COMPANY ENCAMPED HERE BY
MUDDY CREEK FALLS.

MARYLAND HISTORICAL SOCIETY

The Maryland Historical Society at Swallow Falls State Park marking the Vagabonds' camp. Photo courtesy of Wikimedia Commons.

Einstein's Secret Vacation at Deep Creek Lake

M any people consider Albert Einstein the smartest man who ever lived. Yet, when this man who knew almost everything needed to unwind one summer, the vacation spot he chose was Deep Creek Lake.

Einstein vacationed for two weeks in September 1946 at the lake. He was seeking a place where he could find an escape from the unwanted media that wrote about how his scientific theories had led to the creation of the atomic bomb.

John Steiding of Midland invited Einstein to vacation at the lake. Steiding was a chemist at the Celanese plant and came to know Einstein through a co-worker's wife, who was sculpting the great man's bust. "Einstein, who wasn't very tall, found it uncomfortable to pose for the artwork since his feet would not touch the floor. John Steiding, being a handyman, made a footstool for Einstein," according to Francis Tam in an article called "Einstein in Western Maryland."

Besides being able to relax out of the national spotlight for a while, Einstein was also able to have Dr. Frank Wilson examine him for an aneurysm of the aorta of the abdomen.

Einstein stayed at Wilson's lake cottage, the Mar-Jo-Lodge, for two weeks. "He took daily walks along the lake, frequently stopping to chat with strangers who had no idea who he was. He was sometimes seen fishing and also bird-watching with binoculars. He never skipped a meal, but was a light eater. He drank a lot of water and lemonade; his favorite vegetable was fresh corn-on-the-cob from Garrett County," Tam wrote.

Einstein enjoying sailing on Deep Creek Lake in 1946. Reprinted with permission from the Garrett County Historical Society.

In particular, Einstein loved sailing, either with friends or alone. "During one of his many hours spent on the lake with Steiding, Dr. Einstein remarked that 'here you can get nearer to God,'" reported the *Cumberland News*. At times, "people would realize that he wasn't around, go searching for him, and find him in Harry Muma's little sailboat, 'single-handing,' on the Turkey Neck inlet," according to the Garrett County Historical Society's book, *Deep Creek Lake, Past and Present.*

Robbie Steiding sits on the lap of Albert Einstein during a 1946 he made Deep Creek Lake. Robbie's father, John Steiding of Midland, invited Einstein to vacation at Deep Creek Lake. Courtesy of Steve James.

During a visit, John Steiding's brother, Fred, asked Einstein to explain his famous theory of relativity in amateur's terms.

"'Put it this way,' said Einstein, 'if you sit on a park bench with your sweetheart, an hour seems like a minute. If you sit on a hot stove by mistake, a minute seems like an hour,'" Tam wrote.

Einstein later said that his vacation at Deep Creek Lake was "one of the most restful and zestful vacations."

When his time at the lake ended, Einstein showed himself to be a generous guest giving Blair Thompson, who had attended him during the vacation, a $50 gratuity, which would equate to more than $1,000 today.

Albert Einstein getting some exercise rowing a boat on Deep Creek Lake. Reprinted with permission from the Garrett County Historical Society.

Following the vacation, he was back at work. In October, he wrote the United Nations said the organization should form a world government that maintained peace under the threat of nuclear devastation, according to Ze'ev Rosenkranz in *The Einstein Scrapbook*. Einstein also published his papers on his unified field theory in the 1950s.

To the world, the vacation remained a secret until the *Cumberland News* revealed the story in 1979.

Albert Einstein on a sailboat in Deep Creek Lake. Reprinted with permission from the Garrett County Historical Society.

Deep Creek Lake was Jonas Salk's Refuge From the World

D r. Jonas Salk became famous in 1955 when his vaccine to fight polio began being distributed to children nationwide. Up until then, polio was an infectious viral disease that killed or deformed thousands of people, mostly children, each year. In 1954, the year before the vaccine started being used widely, there were 38,000 new cases of polio reported in the U.S. By 1961, polio cases had dropped ninety-seven percent.

Once Salk became a public figure, his duties often took him away from research to deal with the politics of university work. It turned him into a different person.

One of Salk's three sons, Jonathan, was quoted in *Jonas Salk: A Life*, saying, "My memories of my father are divided into prevaccine and postvaccine. Prevaccine, I have images of a warm guy. I remember sitting on his lap, playing with the hair on his chest.... After that, I have the sense that he wasn't around much anymore, mostly mentally. He just wasn't present in the same way."

Because of that, Deep Creek Lake became almost therapeutic for Jonas. The entire family loved visiting the lake, but it allowed Jonas to reconnect with his prevaccine self.

Mary Reisinger wrote in her article, "The Salk Family at Deep Creek Lake," that it was likely the Wishiks family introduced the Salks to Deep Creek Lake. Not only did the Wishiks own property on the lake, but they were neighbors with the Salk family in Pittsburgh. Another famous doctor, Dr. Benjamin Spock, was also a friends of the Salks and enjoyed spending time on the lake in the 1940s and 1950s.

Dr. Jonas Salk.

The lake became such a treasured getaway for the Salks that they built a summer home on the lake. A short blurb in the *Oakland Republican* on May 30, 1957, reported that the Salk family had purchased property on the lake at Paradise Point earlier in the month. The lot they purchased had a broad lawn that sloped down to the lake. They built a one-story cottage on it to live in during the summer.

"For Peter's [one of Salk's sons] father, Deep Creek Lake was a refuge," Reisinger wrote. "His favorite way to relax was to take their small sailboat out onto the water and spend time there in solitude."

The family had three boats; a motorboat, a small sailboat, and a rowboat they built as a family project.

While knowing they would have a summer home was exciting for the family, they didn't get to use it that first summer because of the demands on Salk's time. As soon as school let out in 1957, the family boarded an ocean liner, crossed the Atlantic, and then toured Europe.

"What may have been described to Donna and the boys as a family trip seemed weighted with social functions," Charlotte DeCroes Jacobs wrote in *Jonas Salk: A Life*.

Their time was packed with event after event, many of them requiring formal dress, which the boys hated. Even though the family was together, much of Salk's time was spent with the event hosts. Other times, they didn't see him at all because he was speaking at symposiums and other events on technical aspects of his research.

Jacobs notes that while some wives may have thrived on the elegance of the events and the attention, "Donna would have preferred to be lying in a hammock at Deep Creek Lake, reading."

That didn't happen that year, though. The Salks didn't return to the U.S. until after Labor Day.

As Salk attempted to deal with the good and bad aspects of his fame, he returned to an idea he had long had of creating an institute. His fame could help him establish one, but among those who offered to help were also those who wanted to control the institute and make their own names with it.

During the summer of 1959, the family returned to their lake house. It was something the entire family looked forward to. The boys got to reunite with friends, some of whom they hadn't seen since the previous summer. "Donna likely hoped to recapture her husband's attention," according to Jacobs.

But Jonas wanted to think and be alone with his thoughts.

"This is being dictated in the quiet of the early morning while sitting in front of our lake cottage," he wrote to a friend. "My eyes rest on a view that induces the kind of serenity one likes to feel even if only from time to time. The quiet of the lake... and the beauty of the hills in the distance make this as close to heaven as I will ever get."

He considered the lake, or a place with a similar setting, as some place where he would like to establish his institute.

"As he gazed at the lake, his spirits rose," Jacobs wrote. "The quest to fulfill his dream began to take the form of a crusade."

While it would eventually become a reality, it wouldn't happen at Deep Creek Lake. It wouldn't even happen during the time the Salks spent their summers at the lake. The Salk Institute for Biological Studies opened in 1963 in La Jolla, California.

In the meantime, the Salks continued enjoying summers at the lake. They water skied, played games, and the Jonathan and Darrell dipped their toes in the acting world, taking part in shows at the Garrett County Playhouse. The Oakland Republican noted Darrell worked as a stage manager for one show, and he and Jonathan had roles in the show, Kiss and Tell.

"They must be singled out and recommended on splendid bits of thespian endeavor. Jonathan is the kid brother who gets into everyone's hair and Darrell is the unfortunate Dexter who almost becomes the fall guy," the *Oakland Republican* noted.

During the summer of 1962, a photographer with *Life*

Magazine took pictures of the family enjoying activities on the lake–swimming, boating, and barbequing. They all had bright smiles. The pictures were part of a large feature on Jonas that ran the following February. The *Oakland Republican* noted that because the lake was mentioned and the photos were so complimentary of lake life, that it brought a lot of positive publicity for the lake.

However, just as Deep Creek Lake had helped inspire Jonas in his creation of a research institute, it almost derailed it, too. The feature in Life not only showed the Salk family vacationing, but it talked about the institute which was nearing its opening. It brought a lot of publicity to researchers who weren't used to being in the limelight like Jonas was by this time.

The Salk Institute in La Jolla, California. Courtesy of the Library of Congress.

Another researcher, Mel Cohn, quote a friend who said, "If I might offer some free public relations counsel to the Salk Institute… let's have less of Salk in the sunset and more of him in the lab with that not-so-fresh white coat."

Luckily, they were all able to come together, and the institute continued to grow and help the world with its findings.

The summer of 1962 also turned out to be the last year the Salks spent at Deep Creek Lake. The following year, they moved to California, where Jonas could continue his research at the Salk Institute.

Jonas died from heart failure at 80 on June 23, 1995, in La Jolla. He is buried at El Camino Memorial Park in San Diego.

Future Nobel Prize Winner Renato Dulbecco was one of the researchers at the institute. He wrote, "The article in Life has profoundly disturbed me, and has left me wondering about the true aims of our undertaking." He said he felt like he was "a rare specimen in a zoo or a circus." His ego was a bit hurt too because he felt it focused the institute solely on Jonas.

Who Killed Frank Olson?

T wo bottles of Cointreau sat on the table in front of Frank Olson. Both were open. Both were the same. He reached out for one of the bottles to pour himself an after-dinner drink. He was relaxing in a cabin with other men who had been forced to attend a three-day retreat at Deep Creek Lake from November 18 to 20, 1953.

Olson was an army veteran who worked at Camp Detrick (now Fort Detrick in Frederick, Maryland) as a bacteriologist and biological warfare scientist.

At some point, he had also become a CIA employee. The CIA had recruited him through Camp Detrick's Special Operations Division, which was researching covert ways to use chemical weapons. Many consider it a hidden CIA research station within Camp Detrick.

Olson hadn't wanted to attend the Deep Creek Lake meeting. He was having doubts about the ethicality of his work. He didn't need to learn about the results of the work in which he was involved at Camp Detrick. He needed to think and clear his mind.

He knew the men he was sharing the large cabin on the lake with. They were members of the Special Operations Division and the CIA. Vincent Ruwet, Olson's division chief and friend, had picked him up at his house and they had driven west to find this somewhat isolated cabin. It was a large, two-story rental cabin, off of Route 219, about thirty yards from Deep Creek Lake and 100 yards from the nearest neighbor.

The invitation to the "Deep Creek Rendezvous" said that a cover story had been given for the meeting. "CAMOU-FLAGE: Winter meeting of script writers, editors, authors, lecturers, sports magazines."

Olson believed they were there to talk about the joint projects of the Special Operations Division and CIA involving things like biological warfare and using drugs for mind control.

Unbeknownst to Olson, this was also a camouflage story to get him and others to the cabin for an experiment.

Frank Olson.

The men enjoyed a hearty dinner on Thursday, November 19, and then settled down in the cabin's living room for after-dinner drinks. Robert Lashbrook, a CIA employee and one of the attendees, poured drinks for eight of the men present. He served the drinks and then poured himself and Sidney

Gottlieb drinks from a separate bottle, although there was still liqueur in the first. If it struck anyone as odd or if anyone even noticed, no one remarked on it. Olson took the drink offered him. It was a simple choice, but one that would cost him his life.

He drank the Cointreau and then lost himself in his own thoughts. Sometime between then and Friday afternoon, Olson and the men were told their drinks had been dosed with lysergic acid diethylamide (LSD), according to the Church Committee report. The men wouldn't have noticed it in the Cointreau because LSD is odorless and colorless. It does have a slightly bitter taste, but the alcohol in the drink would have disguised this.

The men had cause for concern. LSD had been developed in 1938, but its psychedelic properties weren't realized until 1943. Although it is not addictive, it was known to cause delusions, paranoia, and anxiety. The CIA also wanted to know if it could be used for mind control.

When Olson returned home that evening, his wife, Alice, "sensed something was wrong the moment he walked in the door. There was a stiffness in the way he kissed her hello and held her. Like he was doing something mechanical, devoid of any meaning or affection," H. P. Albarelli wrote in *A Terrible Mistake*.

Olson's thoughts now were definitely elsewhere. Later that evening, he admitted to her, "I've made a terrible mistake."

On Monday morning at 7:30 a.m., Olson was waiting for Ruwet when he arrived. Olson admitted his doubts about the work he was doing and said that he wanted to resign.

Olson told his wife later, "I talked to Vin. He said that I didn't make a mistake. Everything is fine. I'm not going to resign.

The next day, Ruwet and Lashbrook convinced Olson to

see a psychiatric doctor in New York. Actually, he was meeting with Harold Abramson, an allergist-pediatrician, who was working with the CIA.

Lashbrook and Olson shared a hotel room on the 13th floor of the Statler Hotel. Early on the morning of November 28, a loud crashing noise woke him up. According to the CIA, Olson threw himself out of the window, committing suicide.

The truth turned out to be something far darker and disturbing.

The doorman at the Statler Hotel in New York City had taken a break early, around 2:30 a.m. on the morning of November 28, 1953, to go for a drink at the nearby Little Penn Tavern. As he turned a corner, he saw something falling through the air.

"It was like the guy was diving, his hands out in front of him, but then his body twisted and he was coming down feet first, his arms grabbing at the air above him," the doorman told Armond Pastore, the hotel's night manager, according to Albarelli Jr.

The body hit a wooden partition shielding work being done by the hotel and then the sidewalk. Frank Olson was dead.

The investigation by the CIA, which Olson worked with as part of the Special Operations Unit at Camp Detrick in Frederick, Maryland, found that Olson had died as "the result of circumstances arising out of [the Deep Creek Lake] experiment," and there was a "direct causal connection between that experiment and his death," according to the CIA's general counsel report, according to *The* (Baltimore) *Sun*.

Although these conclusions had been reached within two weeks of Olson's death, his family was only told that he had died in the course of his work. This allowed the Olson family to collect federal death benefits, while the official results of the death investigation remained classified.

More than 20 years later, a presidential commission investigating CIA activities inside the United States found that an Army scientist had fallen to his death from a hotel room in New York after the CIA had given him LSD in 1953. The Olson family confronted Vincent Ruwet, Olson's division chief and friend, who admitted that the scientist was Frank Olson.

President Gerald Ford meets with members of the Olson Family to apologize for the actions that led to Frank Olson's death. Photo courtesy of Wikimedia Commons.

The family then started on a campaign to fully find out what had happened. President Gerald Ford invited the family to the White House and apologized for the death. The family also received a $750,000 settlement from the government.

However, Olson's sons still weren't satisfied that they knew the truth. They had their father's body exhumed in

1994. A new autopsy found that Olson had suffered a blow to the head before he fell from his hotel window. According to the autopsy report, the wound was suggestive of a homicide.

"The Manhattan district attorney's office opened a homicide investigation in 1996. While they were unable to bring charges, they changed the official cause of death from 'suicide' to 'unknown'," *The Sun* reported.

His family filed a lawsuit against the government in 2012, claiming that the CIA is still holding back records about Olson's death.

"The evidence shows that our father was killed in their custody. They have lied to us ever since, withholding documents and information, and changing their story when convenient," Eric Olson told *The Business Insider*. The lawsuit was dismissed in 2013 when a judge ruled that it had been "filed too late and is barred under an earlier settlement," according to *Bloomberg Business*.

Will the full truth about what happened to Frank Olson ever be known? It remains to be seen how the journey that began in a cabin by the lake will end.

Wormwood, released in 2017, is a documentary miniseries based on Olson's case.

"It now appears that the LSD was administered, at a CIA retreat in Maryland, to discover exactly what Olson knew. When this experiment revealed that he was indeed 'unreliable,' he was taken to New York and disposed of," Michael Ignatieff wrote about Wormwood in *The New York Review.*

Frostburg Engineer Disappears at Deep Creek Lake

D uring a pleasant spring day in 1930, Frostburg City Engineer William Harvey drove to Grantsville and ate lunch with his brother at the National Hotel. Then he drove on to Oakland to do some business.

That was the last anyone ever saw of him.

His car was found on the Glendale Road Bridge over Deep Creek Lake on April 5. His overcoat was found in the car along with this pocketbook, which had $135 in cash and $800 in checks.

But no Harvey.

The water around the bridge was estimated at around 60 feet deep, with the bottom covered with snags and debris. The assumption was that Harvey was probably in the water, although no one knew for sure.

Even as a search was organized, "the wealth of rumor and speculation abroad in the county mounted to legendary proportions," according to the *Cumberland Evening Times*.

Hundreds of people, including many from Frostburg, began searching the woods around the lake. Boats crisscrossed the lake, dragging grappling hooks they thought might snag on the body if it was caught underwater.

"Dynamite charges were exploded in an effort to dislodge the body should it be, as is most commonly believed, on the bottom of the lake," the newspaper reported.

One charge comprised fourteen sticks of dynamite and it

shook the bridge when it detonated. The explosions killed hundreds of fish, which floated to the surface of the lake. Others were thrown onto the shore. Spectators gathered up many of those fish and carried them home in baskets where they would become a future meal.

This is the Glendale Road Bridge near where Frostburg City Engineer William Harvey's car was found. Photo courtesy of the Library of Congress.

Meanwhile, two reports came in from supposed witnesses. A teacher said she saw Harvey boarding a train to Oakland on the day he disappeared. James Spier, the assistant manager of the American Grocery Store at Mechanic and Valley streets in Cumberland, said he saw Harvey pass by his store between 2 p.m. and 3 p.m. on April 4th. Investigators asked if Spier might have been referring to Sheriff William Harvey, who was the Frostburg Harvey's nephew. Spier said the two men didn't look alike, and he was sure it was the Frostburg Harvey.

When it was discovered that Harvey had a doctor's appointment at Johns Hopkins University a short time before his disappearance, people suggested that perhaps he had received bad health news and committed suicide. However, people who knew him said he hadn't been despondent.

Accidental drowning was thought to be a slim possibility because Harvey was an excellent swimmer.

"One school of thought and speculation in Frostburg holds that Mr. Harvey might have suffered violence at the hands of illicit liquor manufacturers in that section, mistaking him for Sheriff Harvey," according to the newspaper. This was discounted because the two men looked nothing alike.

The Frostburg Elks Club, where Harvey was a member, hired divers from Brown Salvage and Derrick Corp. from Baltimore to go into the lake and see if they could find anything on the bottom.

Investigators even searched his office at West Union and Water streets for signs of business problems that might have driven him to suicide. "On the contrary contracts and business agreements for spring work aggregating several thousand dollars were found," according to the *Cumberland Evening Times*.

Even robbery was discounted because of the money and checks that were found in the car.

One thing that investigators did learn that made them think if something happened to Harvey, it wasn't his doing was that he was afraid of death and dying before his time.

The search for Harvey ended after eight days on April 13. No sign of him had been found. The investigation was no closer to discovering what had happened that it had been when it was started.

Police got one final report, which was that someone had seen Harvey in San Francisco at a hotel. However, nothing could be confirmed.

The Frostburg Mayor and Commissioners appointed Max Mathias to fill the vacant post of town engineer on April 29. The following day, a young boy, Sherman Friend, and his sister Mabel were fishing near the Glendale Bridge when they found the body floating in the lake. They notified the police who had an ambulance take it to Oakland. It was described as being in fair condition, given the time it had been in the water. It was believed to have been lodged on the bottom and eventually worked its way free as decomposition gases lifted it. However, given how thoroughly the area around the bridge had been searched, police were at a loss for how it could have been missed.

Although Harvey had drowned, no one knew what had happened or why he had even been on that bridge that day.

His funeral took place at St. John's Episcopal Church in Frostburg, and he was buried in Philos Cemetery in Westernport.

BEFORE THE WATER

Deep Creek Lake Could Have Been Part of the C&O Canal

G arrett County's biggest tourist attraction could have looked very different if the Chesapeake and Ohio Canal had continued past Cumberland. Deep Creek Lake was created from building a dam and allowing creeks and streams, including the creek that gives Deep Creek Lake its name, to fill the valley.

In 1824, the holdings of George Washington's Patowmack Company were ceded to the new C.hesapeake and Ohio Canal Company, which had yet to break ground. The canal's route was still in question. The goal was to reach the Ohio River, which would allow canal boats to travel along the river to the Mississippi River, creating an inland trade route from New Orleans to Georgetown.

The largest challenge to this goal was the Allegheny Mountains. To reach Cumberland, Maryland, required raising a canal boat about 800 feet over 185 miles from Georgetown. To reach McHenry from Cumberland would require raising a boat about 1,900 feet over 45 miles, a greater challenge.

In 1824, four years before the C&O Canal broke ground, U.S. Secretary of War John Calhoun and Col. Isaac Roberdeau, who had assisted Charles L'Enfant in laying out Washington D.C., set out to map a route for the canal.

They left Cumberland on August 26, 1824, traveling the National Road and staying in taverns along the way. They wrote of seeing well-timbered land and beautiful farms along the route, but they eventually left the road and headed south, stopping at the farm of the John McHenry at Buffalo Marsh, which is now at the northern end of Deep Creek Lake.

"This party is now engaged in surveying the head waters of Deep Creek and other branches of the Youghiogheny, and will proceed down that river to Monongahela, and thence to Pittsburg, which they expect to reach by the first of December," the *Maryland Republican* reported on September 9, 1824.

The seal of George Washington's Patowmack Company, which was the forerunner to the Chesapeake and Ohio Canal Company.

The McHenry Family welcomed the surveying party with "that sort of Highland welcome which does a heart good," according to the *Maryland Republican*.

Not far from the farm was the summit level of the canal. According to *The Glades Star*, it was marked on a pier of the old wooden Deep Creek Bridge where present-day Route 219 crosses Deep Creek. The summit level indicated "the high water mark of the storage dam to provide water for lifting and lowering the canal boats thru the locks."

Crews work at repairing a section of the Chesapeake and Ohio Canal. Building the canal and maintaining the canal was labor intensive, requiring work crews using horses and mules for power. Photo courtesy of the National Park Service.

The group went to a spot about a quarter mile below the bridge along Deep Creek. There they erected two dams a short distance apart and opened and closed them at certain times to see if Deep Creek had enough water to fill a lock sixty feet long, twelve feet wide, and ten feet deep in thirteen minutes. The tests were done three times, and each time was a success. The newspaper noted that this was during the dry season, and there had been no rain for forty days, and "Buffalo Marsh Run which fed into Deep Creek was lower than hunters could remember," according to the *Maryland Republican*.

"But should even Deep Creek, and all its branches, be

found insufficient to furnish water enough for Canal naviga-
tion, it is reduced to a certainty that the waters of both the
Youghiogheny's can be brought to the summit level, which
forever settles the question of water," the newspaper reported.

It was proposed that a twenty-one-foot dam on the Little
Youghiogheny and a thirty-five-foot dam on the Big Youghiogheny would be needed to provide enough water for a canal
to operate through present-day Garrett County.

A canal boat is towed along the Chesapeake and Ohio Canal,
which runs roughly parallel to the Potomac River from
Georgetown, Maryland, to Cumberland, Maryland. Photo
courtesy of the National Park Service.

"And Deep Creek that now moves along unseen and but
little known shall become famous as the stream of Washington, for its waters will mingle with those of the Potomac and
pass the shades of Mt. Vernon where he who first formed the
grand design of uniting the waters of the West and the East...
now rests in peace. From this summit level the waters of
Deep Creek shall find a sea on either side. Flowing westward
it will pass the spot (by way of the Ohio and Mississippi)

where Jackson saved his country and gained immortal fame.

About two miles from the summit level, the surveying group found," the *Maryland Advocate* opined.

The newspaper also noted that it believed Calhoun had been sold on the idea and that construction should start and use that route.

Although the C&O Canal broke ground on July 4, 1828, it never reached present-day Deep Creek Lake or the Ohio River. It stopped at Cumberland after reaching there in 1850.

Where the Buffalo Roamed

I n the early 1700s, before White settlers had pushed their way westward over the mountains, Native American tribes would visit the area of present-day Garrett County to partake in an activity that still continues there today... hunting.

Their hunting was different back then, even for them. They had spears and arrows, which was fine for most game. However, the reason they came to the area was to hunt buffalo. For them, the Native Americans probably used atlatl, a device used to throw a spear that increased its speed and distance.

"Bison appear to have been less abundant east of the Appalachian Mountains and rare within the forested mountains," according to the National Park Service. "An Englishman first reported bison near the Potomac River in 1612."

These weren't the North American Bison, which are often called buffalo because of their resemblance to buffalo in Africa. The East Wood Bison was slightly smaller than their western cousins and they had a hump in the middle of their backs.

"With black wrinkled skin during the hot summers and long shaggy hair in the winter, their hair often fell over their eyes, obstructing their view," the Frederick News Post reported.

Although East Wood Bison were a popular quarry for Native Americans, Europeans also hunted them. They provided plenty of meat and their hides were a great material for shelter and clothing. The bison also made it fairly easy to find them. Not only were they one of the larger animals people hunted, they traveled the same paths back and forth. "Well worn bison trails, called 'traces' were commonly used for human travel, as they extended for many miles. Many became routes for today's roads and railroads," according to the National Park Service.

The picture shows a wood bison, a cousin of the American bison. Wood bison lived in the eastern U.S. up to 1940, and like their cousins, are often referred to as buffalo. Courtesy of Wikimedia Commons.

As the Native Americans hunted the buffalo during the summer, they realized their weapons were not as effective as they should be. Even if they struck the buffalo with an arrow or spear, it was difficult to make a fatal shot through the buffalo's thick fur.

Thomas A. Glotfelty wrote in his book, Mountain Mist, that the hunters drove the buffalo toward a marsh area that they had filled with bush and firewood.

"As the herd approached the marsh, the tribe members would stampede the buffalo by waving robes and garments and setting the piles of brush on fire," Ed King wrote in *Deep Creek Lake: The Founders.*

This action funneled the buffalo into the muddy marsh and water. It slowed them down, allowing the hunters to catch them. The animals couldn't escape the hunters easily and were killed.

It is this use of the marsh, which led white settlers to name the area Buffalo Marsh later.

George Washington also knew of the buffalo that were in the area. During a 1784 trip to look over lands in the west, he was returning to Mount Vernon and decided to make a side trip. He sent part of his group on to Mount Vernon, but he, his nephew, Bushrod Washington, and their servants started eastward on McCullough's Path. This was an Indian path that went from the Winchester, Virginia, area across present-day Garrett County to the headwaters of the Ohio River.

On Sept. 25, the group arrived "at the entrance of the Yohiogany glades." This is believed to have been somewhere near Swallow Falls. Unfortunately, a heavy shower dumped rain on them, and they had nothing but their cloaks to cover them. The following day, he wrote that they were following "McCullocks path, which owes its origin to the buffaloes…"

The National Park Service estimates that at one time two to four million bison were east of the Mississippi, but just like their western cousins, the East Wood Bison are now gone. They were declared extinct in 1940, yet their memory remains because early settlers names towns and geographic features after them. East of the Mississippi, you can find places names Buffalo River, Buffalo Mountain, and in Garrett County, Buffalo Marsh.

William Wilton Ashby and his family were the first permanent settlers in the Great Glades area of Garrett County in the 1780s. Bison were present during the early years of the settlement they established.

William's wife, Sarah, told stories of how at night members of the settlement they established saw Native Americans watching their homes. Not sure of the Native Americans' intentions, the White settlers threw buffalo tallow on the fires to make the fire quickly grow larger and give the impression that more people were in the settlement that there actually were.

Once, during the winter, one of the Ashbys and a neighbor went hunting some of the neighbor's cows that had wandered off. They followed tracks they saw until they found wooly hair snagged on a branch.

"Have your cows grown wool?" Ashby asked.

"They have been gone so long, damned if I know what they have grown," the neighbor replied.

They continued following the train, and eventually came up four bison. They shot the bulls, but the cows escaped to the west.

According to *The Glades Star*, these were the last buffalo seen in the Glades.

It's the place where buffalo roamed and died. Their bones may still be buried in the mud beneath McHenry Cove in Deep Creek Lake, which now covers Buffalo Marsh.

Where McHenry Got Its Name

W hen people hear the name McHenry, they often associate it with Fort McHenry, the Baltimore fort that withstood a British bombardment during the War of 1812 and inspired Francis Scott Key to write the poem that would eventually become our national anthem. However, on the other side of Maryland, people associate the name with the Garrett County town next to Deep Creek Lake. The interesting thing is they are both named for the same person, James McHenry.

James McHenry was in Ballymena, Ireland, in 1753, and he got his early education in Dublin. He immigrated to the colonies in 1771, arriving in Baltimore. His father, Daniel, and brother, John, followed him later. They opened a mercantile store in Baltimore called Daniel McHenry and Son.

James had higher aspirations. He went to Philadelphia and studied medicine under Dr. Benjamin Rush, who is considered one of the country's Founding Fathers.

When the Revolutionary War broke out, James served as a doctor at a hospital in Cambridge. He was then appointed as a surgeon to Col. Robert Magaw's Fifth Pennsylvania Battalion. Acting against Commander-in-Chief General George Washington's orders to abandon Fort Washington in 1776, Magaw, acting commander of the fort, thought he could defend it against the British.

During the Battle of Fort Washington on November 16, James was captured. Two months later, he returned to Baltimore. About a year later, he was formally exchanged, and shortly thereafter, he was appointed to serve as Washington's secretary.

According to *The Glades Star*, "...when he took the oath of allegiance in June before Gen. Nathaniel Greene, he terminated his short career in the field of medicine. He was never known to practice again."

James McHenry. Photo courtesy of Wikimedia Commons.

During his time with Washington, the two became friends. Near the end of the war, James served for a time as a major on Gen. Lafayette's staff in 1781.

Once American had won its independence, James entered

politics and was elected to the Maryland Senate in September 1781. Three years later, he became a Maryland Congressional Representative. Then, in 1787, he was appointed one of Maryland's delegates to the Constitutional Convention, which drafted the U.S. Constitution. He was elected to the Maryland House of Delegates in 1788.

He withdrew from public life for a time because of the death of his brother, John. In a letter to Washington, James wrote, "Every sorrow and consideration has been swallowed up in the depth of affliction I have felt on the loss of my brother…" Later in the letter, he added, "For some years I have entertained an aversion to public life… and this aversion has been increased by my brother's death. I intend to devote the remainder of my life to my own ease, to my devotions, the recollection of a dear brother, the happiness of my family, and literary amusements."

Despite this, in 1791, he accepted another term in the Maryland Senate and served for the next five years.

During Washington's second term as president, he chose his Secretary of War Timothy Pickering to serve as his secretary of state. This meant he needed a new secretary of war. After Washington's first three choices declined to serve as the new secretary, Washington called on his old friend and secretary. James accepted and became the third secretary of war for the United States.

As the secretary of war, he pushed Congress to maintain a strong military. He also pushed for training academies for the Army and Navy. He also tried to the keep the military ready for a second war with Britain.

During President John Adam's term as president, James continued to serve as secretary of war, although he and Adams frequently disagreed to the point where Adams asked for his resignation. James submitted it in May 1800.

Soon after, the new fort defending Baltimore was named after a native son and recent secretary of war, James McHenry. James first visited Western Maryland to his friend, Col. John Lynn, who served as the first Allegany County Clerk of Court.

He and another friend bought 13,056 acres of the Deep Creek Glades in 1808. Two years later, James bought 444 acres of Locust Tree Bottom tract, and finally, in 1812, he bought John Lynn's half of the Wild Cherry Tree Meadows tract. He was a major landowner in what was then western Allegany County.

Although he owned property and a home in Western Maryland, James maintained his home in Ridgely's Delight, a Baltimore neighborhood where future baseball legend Babe Ruth would be born.

He often spent his summers away from the Baltimore heat, enjoying the cooler temperatures of western Allegany County. Because of health problems, he also spent the entire winter of 1812-1813 at his Western Maryland home because he was unable to travel back to Baltimore.

James's wife, Peggy, wrote, "Where there [Cherry Tree Meadows] my dear husband was taken with an infirmity in his legs, which, notwithstanding every means was used for his relief, gradually increased until he was entirely deprived of the use of them. The winter then coming on, we were obliged to remain there till the following summer when with great difficulty he was got home."

He died in 1816 at age sixty-two. His nephew, John McHenry, inherited some of this uncle's land and moved his family to the region to establish the first permanent home in Cherry Tree Meadows, according to the *Oakland Republican*.

It was not easy because the area was wilderness mostly. "Housekeeping was difficult; coffee, tea, sugar, and any materials for clothing were purchased in Baltimore, and brought by wagon from Cumberland. Bacon and flour were brought from Uniontown," according to the *Republican*.

During John's lifetime, the settlement slowly grew as more families moved west. John built a new log home at Buffalo Marsh. It had a barn, smokehouse, hen house, and cattle shed. Another home was built later to replace that one and be near the county road when it was constructed. A big red gate on the end of the property held a sign that read: "McHenry's Gate." Because of frequent reference to it, it became the unofficial name of the community.

Margaret Caldwell McHenry. Photo courtesy of Wikimedia Commons.

When the U.S. Post Office opened in the area on February 22, 1875, the first postmaster, William Casteel, officially named the community McHenry.

James is buried at what is now the Westminster Hall and Burying Ground. One of the other notable people buried in this small cemetery is Edgar Allan Poe. However, John McHenry and his wife are buried in unmarked graves in an old orchard near their home.

Part of the original Cherry Tree Meadow tract is now underwater in Deep Creek Lake.

Is There Lost Treasure Near Deep Creek Lake?

W hile Deep Creek Lake is considered a Garrett County treasure, it's not typically what springs to mind when someone mentions treasure in the county. And honestly, neither is silver and gold. Yet there are stories that indicate the northern county region might be hiding more than one lost treasure.

Layman's lost silver

In the early 1800s, George Layman went out hunting one day in what is now northern Garrett County. At the time, Garrett County was still part of Allegany County. He walked for quite some time, heading south and west toward what is now Deep Creek Lake. He searched for game that seemed to have abandoned the area. At some point, he realized that not much around him was looking familiar. He was lost.

Back then, you couldn't whip out a cell phone and call up a map or call for help. You couldn't even walk and hope to reach a paved road. There just weren't many roads around.

So Layman started walking in the direction he thought was home, but it was still quite a hike.

"Tired and thirsty, he came at last to a free-flowing mountain spring. After quenching his thirst and while resting beside the spring, he noticed an outcropping of rock that was like nothing he had ever seen before," an article by Ross C. Durst in *Tableland Trails* noted.

The rock had a metallic sheen to it, and when he broke off a piece, it was heavier than he expected. He shoved it into his pocket and started walking again.

He made it back home and forgot all about the curious rock that he had found. He set it on a shelf and allowed neighbors to be surprised by its appearance.

One friend was more than surprised, though. He convinced Layman to have the rock assayed. Layman agreed, and it turned out that there was silver in the rock. It was extracted and minted into coins that would be worth around $270 today.

"Daniel Layman, son of George and the writer's uncle, carried one of these silver half-dollars as a pocket-piece during most of his life," Durst noted.

Knowing that his rock had been only a piece of a much larger stone, Layman tried to find the original rock once again. He did remember the farm that he finally recognized after being lost. It was located about five miles from the National Road at New Germany below Twin Churches. However, that was the only point he knew for certain.

"The lapse of time had erased most of the details and the face of nature had changed," Durst wrote. "Nature seems to have exposed her secret for a moment then dropped the curtain. A century later, her secret is still undisclosed."

After years of unsuccessfully searching for the outcropping on his own, Layman told his family of the only clues that he could remember. One was that the stream next to the rock had been flowing east and that he believed the spring had been on the west side of Meadow Mountain.

Durst said these clues actually narrowed the search because relatively few of the springs on the west side of the mountain flowed east. However, no amount of searching has ever yielded a silver lode.

"If the lode is ever discovered it will probably be entirely accidental just as was the original discovery," Durst wrote.

The Silver Belle Mine

The story of Layman's lost silver vein is believed to have attracted a pair of prospectors from Arizona who came into northern Garrett County searching for silver.

When they discovered silver on the farm of Hiram Duckworth, they decided to form a mining company for a mine they named the Silver Belle and issued stock to raise capital to extract the silver. Their company, the Silver Belle Mining Company of Garrett County, was incorporated in West Virginia and capitalized for $250,000 with shares selling for $5.

Bankers in Lonaconing invested heavily in the mine and Georges Creek coal miners were hired to mine the silver.

The problem was when they went to work, they found no paying ore.

The mine eventually failed, and the finger pointing began, but it seems that the original miners had used the story of Layman's lost mine as a stock-selling scheme.

It was many years after Layman's discovery that silver was found again. In 1890, silver was found in Bear Pen Hollow, which is on the upper part of the Savage River Gorge. Sam Miller and another man found the silver seam and opened a mining operation.

Miners descended on ladders into the shaft and could then mine on several different levels. However, the operation ran only a few months before the silver seam petered out, and the mine was abandoned.

Some believe that there still might be silver in the area because they believe the company owners did not know how to do hard-rock mining properly. Others think the mine may have been salted as part of a stock-selling scheme.

The Duckworth Mine

About eight miles away from the Silver Belle, another mine was opened in the Black Lick Run Hollow area. This was a private mine on property owned by Israel Duckworth.

The story goes that Mrs. Duckworth "dreamed three nights in succession that silver would be found by digging beside a certain log in the woods with which she was familiar," according to *The Glades Star.*

Although the ore samples initially showed a good grade of silver, much like the Silver Belle Mining Company, the seam petered out too quickly.

Victor Harvey wrote in *The Glades Star*, "First, it is true that there really is silver in Garrett County. To what extent is not known."

He drew this conclusion from speaking with many of the old timers in the county.

He said samples assayed all supposedly showed lower-quality silver than the Layman lode, which is believed to have been the first silver found in the county.

Braddock's lost gold

Somewhere between Cumberland, Maryland, and Pittsburgh, Pennsylvania, a chest of gold coins lies hidden with what could amount to a couple million dollars in gold today. It is buried beneath a tree at the confluence of two rivers according to the only survivor of the men who hid the chest from French soldiers and Indian warriors in 1755.

And yet no one has found it.

The fact and the legend, obfuscated by more than 250 years, have led treasure hunters for years to wonder "Where is General Braddock's lost gold?"

General Edward Braddock left Fort Cumberland on June 6, 1755, heading toward Fort Duquesne in western Pennsylvania. Their route took them through what is now northern Garrett County, along a route roughly parallel to the National Road. Along this section of their journey, they made four camps.

The difficult terrain of steep mountain ridges and thick forests slowed their progress. Braddock's aide, George Washington, recommended splitting the army so that the best men could rush ahead and reach their destination while the rest of the army with the supplies would make its best time.

The gold was among the supplies. It was payroll money for the army. It would have also been used to pay Indians as guides and to keep them peaceful. Washington had brought it to Fort Cumberland from Williamsburg, Virginia, just before the army left.

When the army left Fort Cumberland is the last verifiable account of the gold.

A month later, Indians working with the French attacked the British. Around 500 soldiers were killed, another 500 wounded, and just 300 survived without harm. Braddock was among the dead.

Only twenty-eight Indians and Frenchmen were killed in the attack.

The gold was never seen again.

Legend says that before getting involved in the expected battle at Fort Duquesne, Braddock ordered the gold buried to keep it from the French. The plan was to recover it after the battle was won.

Braddock held a council among his officers and asked them to wait until after the battle to get paid. They would not be able to spend the gold before then, and because casualties were expected in the fighting, there would be fewer men to divide the gold among after the battle.

The men agreed, and six soldiers transported the gold to a

68

location at the confluence of two rivers and buried the chest under a walnut tree.

Shortly after that, Braddock was killed, and the remainder of the army retreated. No one ever returned to claim the gold.

Indians working with the French attacked and killed General Braddock's men. The British troops were on their way to Fort Duquesne with a payroll chest, but buried it before they were massacred. Photo courtesy of the Library of Congress.

A story recounted in *Incredible, Strange, Unusual...* by Harold Scott recounts a story from May 1881. A Cumberland man driving a horse and wagon along the National Road, which was built along Braddock's army route, was about 30 miles west of Cumberland. This would have been around Keyser's Ridge, Maryland, or near what is called the Bear Camp for Braddock's Army.

The Cumberland man saw an old man holding a crowbar. The man stopped his horse to watch the old man. The old man said he was a descendant of one of the men who had buried Braddock's gold. The story passed down through his family was that the chest was buried where a large rock divided two streams. Members of his family had been trying to find the gold since Braddock's defeat.

In October 1941, rain washed Allegany County for three days. After it had ended, a hiker found a British coin on the road. The coin was close to a mountainside where water was still running off from the rainfall. Thinking the coin may have come from further up the mountain, the man began exploring and found another British coin. Though he searched for more on different occasions, the treasure eluded him.

Other rumors have appeared about the gold. In the 1950's, it was believed that the gold was buried where Crawford Run flows into the Youghiogheny River.

One story hypothesizes that the gold is still in Virginia in Fairfax County. Charles Gilliss wrote about his theory in 1954 that because Braddock was having trouble moving his men and supplies through Virginia's wilderness, he left some things behind. Among the items were two, small brass cannons that had been filled with gold and capped with wooden plugs. Gilliss said the cannons were buried "two feet beneath the soil, fifty paces East of a spring, where the road runs North and South."

This account has been discredited, though, because Braddock and his army never came near the Centreville, Virginia.

Others believe that the French were able to recover the chest themselves and took it as spoils of war, though no one ever claimed credit for it.

Six soldiers buried a chest of gold before being massacred along with General Braddock's troops. The location of the treasure is now the stuff of legends. Photo courtesy of the Library of Congress.

Garrett had Another Large Lake Before Deep Creek Lake

M aryland has no natural lakes, which makes Deep Creek Lake that much more impressive. However, before Garrett County was home to the state's largest lake, a businessman created another lake in the county that was impressive for its time.

In 1921, the *Cumberland Daily News* reported on a 75-acre lake that could be seen from the National Road midway between Grantsville and Keyser's Ridge.

James Todd was the wealthy head of Sterling Varnish Works in Haysville, Pennsylvania. The company opened in 1894 and eventually acquired twenty-one patents for its products and processes. In fact, one set of proprietary processes for creating varnish was called the "Todd Processes," named after Todd.

Todd had spent a lot of time during his youth hunting and fishing in the region, and once he was successful and wealthy, he wanted to create a hunting and fishing preserve where he could continue enjoying his hobbies and get away from the stress of his work.

However, it also required him to get away from the Pittsburgh area where he lived. He and his wife, Louise, had a home in Sewickley, a town about 12 miles northwest of Pittsburgh, along the Ohio River. The beautiful home built in 1902 boasted elaborate woodwork so that the beauty and durability of his varnishes could be used. It still stands today and was on the market in 2023 for $2.85 million.

Todd was just as elaborate in building his getaway as he was building his home. He purchased the 500-acre Peter Royer Farm. While it had fields, woodlands, and good water, Todd wanted more. He decided he wanted a lake where he could fish from the shore or take a boat into the water and fish in deeper water.

The section of the National Road that passes closest to Lake Louise. Photograph by the Maryland State Roads Commission. Courtesy of the Enoch Pratt Free Library, Central Library/State Library Resource Center, Baltimore, Maryland

He made plans for the lake and spent a year constructing it, clearing the area that would be filled and building a dam to capture water from nearby streams. The primary watering source for the lake was Puzzley Run.

At the time, a stone bridge the National Road spanned Puzzley Run, which is named for Benjamin Pussley, who lived in the area in the late 1700s. However, the road was relocated in 1932. According to the Maryland Roads Commission, "Early 19th century engineers designed roads so that bridges could be built over them at right angles, which was the cheapest and most efficient manner. This led to the existence of sharp curves just before and after bridges. The old bridge, which is almost invisible from the road today, has deteriorated considerably since this photograph was taken."

The lake, which became Lake Louise, was located 2,800 feet above sea level. When it was built, it was one of the largest lakes in the Allegheny Mountains.

To create a place where he could pursue his hobbies, Todd had the lake stocked with 5,000 trout. He also had it "equipped with every device to protect the small fish from the larger ones," according to the *Cumberland Daily News*. A net was also placed over the spillway to keep the fish in the lake.

Once the lake was filled, Todd spent many of his weekends on the lake often bringing his friends to fish and hunt.

The lake also attracted the attention of municipal officials who were considering how to create water supplies for their towns. The newspaper noted that officials from Cumberland and Frostburg visited the lake, studying how it was created and how it thrived. Frostburg officials considered making a deal to use it as a way to enlarge the city's water supply.

The uniqueness of such a large lake in Garrett County moved from Lake Louise to Deep Creek Lake when it was created in 1925.

Building a Lake

A lthough Deep Creek Lake is a beautiful place with fishing, swimming, and boating, many people don't know that the lake was created as a way to generate electricity.

It was also supposed to be part of a larger project of four lakes in Garrett County. Besides a dam on Deep Creek near its confluence with the Youghiogheny River, there was a second dam to be further north on the Youghiogheny River, and two dams further south. They were designated the Deep Creek, Sang Run, Swallow Falls, and Crellin dams.

Planning for the lakes began in 1920 with surveying, engineering, and purchasing the needed land. With the land purchases came fifty buildings, including two schools and a grange hall. "In some cases, whole farms were purchased when only a part of them was to be flooded, and in a few instances it was found necessary to purchase farms which were not even reached by the inundating water because access to them was cut off by the abandonment of roads or parts of roads," according to *The Glades Star*.

Groundbreaking for the lake was on November 1, 1923, and construction on the dam and powerhouse began a month later. By this time, over 8,000 acres of land had been purchased for a single lake impounded behind the Deep Creek Dam. It was envisioned as an eighty-six-foot-tall dam that spanned 1,340 feet across the river. The powerhouse had two 12,000-horsepower generators.

For such a large project that would be a major economic

driver in the county for the next two years, the groundbreaking was not reported on in the *Oakland Republican.*

The original location of the dam was 750 feet upstream from where it was actually constructed, according to *The Glades Star.* "The impoundment dam was an earth-filled dam with a concrete center," *The Glades Star* reported.

The electricity generated by water passing through turbines at the powerhouse would then be transmitted through power lines to Pennsylvania.

Construction of the Deep Creek Lake hydroelectric dam in September 1924. Photo courtesy of the Library of Congress.

This construction required temporary infrastructure to support it. A narrow-gauge rail line called a "dinky" was built from Oakland to the powerhouse construction site. It was used to bring materials brought in on the Baltimore and Ohio Railroad north to the construction site. A quarry was opened that had a large stone crusher to prepare stone needed in the construction. Two work camps were constructed to house the 1,000 workers needed to build the dam and power- house. Seven miles of wagon roads were built to allow wag- ons to carry materials needed to build the transmission lines.

Teams of horses dragged poles that would hold the transmission lines along the wagon roads to where they were needed. George Browning worked with the horses erecting the poles. *The Glades Star* recounted a story from him of when the horses were too sick to work, so he used his cars to drag the poles over the fields in order to stay on schedule.

Construction of the Deep Creek Lake hydroelectric dam. On the left, you can see a steam engine that carried supplied from Oakland on a B&O Railroad spur line that ran through what is now the Oakland Golf Course, Round Glade, and the Red Run area. The spur was known as the "Dinky Track." Reprinted with permission from the Garrett County Histori- cal Society.

In another story *The Glades Star* recounted was from Milton Sincell. He was on the engineering staff for the lake.

His bosses told him to go to Rochester, New York, to meet the train carrying the transformer for the powerhouse and stay with it until it arrived at the powerhouse construction site.

It took him two days to find the transformer in New York. He rode in freight train cabooses behind the transformer as it traveled to Oakland. This trip took ten days because the freight train had to keep switching lines, but it finally arrived in Oakland.

From there, it was transferred onto a rail car on the dinky line. Half a dozen people crowded with him into the train engine cab to travel to the powerhouse and help unload the transformer there.

"Near Miller's Run, someone looked back and cried, 'the transformer's gone!' Immediately everyone else looked back... and sure enough the railroad car with the transformer wasn't there," Sincell told *The Glades Star*.

They backed the engine up, searching for the decoupled rail car. They were surprised to see it rolling towards them. They got the engine moving forward to avoid a collision.

"Finally we came to a slight grade, and the transformer car began to slow down," Sincell said.

They were trying to figure out how to re-couple the rail car when Frank Browning jumped down and put an axe handle behind the wheels of the transformer rail car. Then he set the hand brake on the car and slowly backed up the engine until they could re-couple.

Some permanent infrastructure was also built. This included new roads and bridges that would be needed once the lake was filled.

During the construction, Deep Creek continued to flow through an outlet in the dam. However, once the construction was completed, the outlet was closed, and the lake began to form in March 1925.

"Very slowly water began to accumulate at the foot of the impoundment dam that had been under construction for over a year, and Deep Creek Lake was born," according to *The Glades Star.*

The original project had been that it would take six months for the lake to fill, but heavy rains and snows accelerated the schedule, and the powerhouse went active on May 26, 1925. The final cost of the project was over $9 million.

Although Garrett County plans to celebrate the centennial anniversary of Deep Creek Lake in 2025, no mention of the power plant coming online was made in the *Oakland Republican* in May 1924.

The power Deep Creek Lake generates is used solely in western Pennsylvania from the Maryland border north to Lake Erie.

Construction of the Deep Creek Lake hydroelectric dam showing the spur line that carried supplies from Oakland in the foreground. Reprinted with permission from the Garrett County Historical Society.

The temporary infrastructure slowly disappeared. The work camps were dismantled. The quarry closed. The railroad removed. Writing in *The Glades Star*, John Grant said that two Rio buses owned by Gorman Thayer and Cecil Ramsay, that were used to transport workers to work sites for the lake, found a new use, transporting students to school for another ten years.

Here Comes the Water

P eople knew something was happening. They had seen surveyors working around McHenry for months. Some people had even put the pieces together to figure out the project. They just couldn't wrap their heads around the scope of the project. Then the Associated Press on November 21, 1923, announced that a new lake would be formed in Garrett County. As the *Oakland Republican* declared the following day, "Gigantic Power Project Near Oakland Planned."

The Associated Press announcement came after the projected had been presented to the Maryland Public Service Commission for its approval. "For upwards of eighteen months a corps of engineers under the direction of Mr. F. H. Corliss, chief, has been engaged in running lines along the streams north of Oakland, including Youghiogheny River, Deep Creek and their numerous tributaries," the *Republican* reported.

By harnessing the power of the rivers and creeks in the area, hydroelectric power would be generated and sold to the Penn Public Service Company for distribution throughout Western Pennsylvania.

"The plan prepared by Charles B. Hawley, construction engineer of the Youghiogheny River Power Company and the Youghiogheny Water and Electric Company, contemplates the development of approximately 100,000 horsepower and the construction of a controlled water power dam and tunnel," the *Republican* reported. The Youghiogheny Company had considered building four major dams and three powerhouses at Deep Creek, Sang Run, Swallow Falls, and Crellin, according to Stephen Schlosnagle in *Garrett County: A History of Maryland's Tableland.*

Construction was planned to begin at the point where Deep Creek flowed into the Youghiogheny River. A seventy-foot-tall dam that would be 1,200 feet wide was planned for construction across the creek.

Construction began on December 1, 1923, after more than 8,000 acres of land had been purchased.

An aerial view of part of Deep Creek Lake. Photo courtesy of the Instantstreetview.com.

David Forney, writing in *The Glades Star*, noted that the original location of the dam was 750 feet upstream from where it was actually constructed. "The impoundment dam was an earth-filled dam with a concrete center," *The Glades Star* reported. Once built, it impounded the water from the surrounding creeks.

"Very slowly water began to accumulate at the foot of the impoundment dam that had been under construction for over a year, and Deep Creek Lake was born," according to *The Glades Star.*

The lake began filling in March 1925. It had originally been thought that it would take at least six months to fill, but heavy rains and snows sped up the schedule.

John Grant also wrote how nine miles of state and county roads had to be rerouted as the water rose. One section of road was near the Point View Inn. "Each week as we passed the area, we would notice how close the encroaching water was to the old state road. Gradually it covered the road and the bridge as it got higher and higher. For a week or so, only the three-foot-high side walls of the structure could be seen; then they also disappeared under the lake's surface," Grant wrote.

After roughly two years of construction and filling, the result was the 1.5-mile-long Deep Creek Lake is filled with 7.7 million cubic feet of water and is 2,340 feet above sea level. The powerhouse went active on May 26, 1925. The final cost of the project was $9 million.

Although Deep Creek Lake was considered the culmination of a twenty-year dream, people had considered building a large man-made lake in the county since 1823. Back then, it would have been used to supply water to the planned-for Chesapeake and Ohio Canal on its way to the Ohio River, which never reached that far.

James Shriver led the party of engineers. He wrote, "It is stated that after the usual thaws in the spring of the year, and melting of heavy snows which commonly fall in this quarter, an inundation is produced, which covering the flat lands for many miles along Deep Creek, produces a lake of considerable extent."

Deep Creek Lake served its purpose, providing the generation of power for the electric company, but it also became a tourist attraction for Garrett County and a Maryland treasure.

Stacked Lakes

I f you were asked what is beneath the water in Deep Creek Lake, you might think of mud, vegetation, and debris from buildings that used to be on the properties that make up the lake bed. One thing you probably wouldn't answer is lakes.

Two lakes lie under Deep Creek Lake. They became part of Deep Creek Lake when Deep Creek was dammed in 1923. Like Deep Creek Lake, they were also artificial lakes.

Lake Cleveland

Gus W. Delawder, a long-time Garrett County resident and former Burgess of Oakland, became Maryland's Commissioner of Fisheries for the region west of Baltimore in 1883. One of the early problems he faced was the declining fish population in state waterways.

"Growing human populations and expanding settlements had polluted waterways. Abusive logging of forests with no thought of regeneration and poor farming practices created conditions for mass erosion," Champ Zumbrun wrote in his article, "Aquaculture comes to Maryland." "These poor agricultural practices resulted in massive deposits of sediment and silt into waterways, destroying fish habitat. Neither catch limits nor environmental laws were yet in place to protect fish habitat or keep waters clean from mills, factories, and towns. Standard practices allowed the dumping of raw sewage and industrial wastes from mills and factories into rivers."

Delawder promoted creating a "pisciculture" program

modeled after a similar program in New York. Today, we call this aquaculture, and the program established fish hatcheries where fish could be raised in controlled conditions and then released into the waterways.

With the help of Maryland Gov. Oden Bowie and Robert Roosevelt (Theodore Roosevelt's uncle), a plan was developed for Maryland, and Garrett County was chosen as the location for the hatchery.

Delawter purchased 1,000 acres around the area where Deep Creek and Cherry Creek meet, not far from the present-day Thayerville Cemetery on Route 219. The creeks were dammed and a mile-long lake formed that was a quarter mile wide at its widest. According to *The Baltimore Sun*, the lake covered forty-five acres. The lake reached depths of up to ten feet deep. *The Sun* said the lake had "water the color of weak coffee."

It was named Lake Cleveland in honor of President Grover Cleveland, who took a break from his honeymoon at Deer Park to spend a day fishing on the lake in 1886.

And fishing was good on the lake. Delawder stocked it with between 50,000 and 60,000 fish annually, which included brook trout, rainbow trout, and landlocked salmon. Fishermen were hooking trout that weighed more than three pounds.

"Deep creek is said to be the best trout stream in the Alleghanies, and doubtless Mr. Delawder, with his experience in fish culture, will make this one of the grandest places for sportsmen in the mountains," *The Sun* reported.

Not only was it a great place to fish, it also turned out to be a great place to hunt water fowl.

"During the snowstorm on Saturday, the lake was literally covered with wild ducks and other water fowl, of which Mr. Delawder bagged a goodly number," according to *The Sun.*

To top it off, Delawder built a lodge on the lake, which was called the Deep Creek Lodge. Reports said the lodge had eight rooms and a wide porch. Outbuildings included an ice house, a buggy house, and a large garden, so guests could enjoy fresh vegetables along with their fish.

President Grover Cleveland and his new bride fishing in the lake that would be named after him as the media writes up news stories. Courtesy of the White House Historical Association.

"Delawder assembled the building in a unique way using only nuts and bolts, not using a single nail," Zumbrun wrote.

Sportsmen would rent rooms at the lodge and get their fill of fishing and hunting. He even had a twenty-foot by five-foot steam-powered boat constructed for the lake, which he named Frankie.

The lake was a success, and by 1889, the *Cumberland Daily Times* noted that people were building summer homes on the lake.

Delawder also bought property about a mile away from Lake Cleveland to create a second lake eventually.

Lake Brown

In 1892, Richard T. Browning, the grandson of western Maryland frontiersman, Meshach Brown, took over as the Maryland Commissioner of Fisheries from his friend, Gus Delawder. Browning was a Civil War veteran who had served in both the Maryland House and Senate for thirteen years.

Browning then oversaw the construction of a second lake, which was originally identified as State Lake and was re-named Lake Brown after Governor Frank Brown. The lake was about a mile long and 200 to 300 yards wide, and it reached depths up to fifteen feet. It was located south of the present-day Glendale Bridge. The lake and the dam can be found on a 1913 map published by the Maryland Department of Forest and Parks.

"Lake Brown on Deep Creek may be one of the first publically funded Maryland state projects for the sole purpose of providing public access for fishing and outdoor recreation," Ed King wrote in *Deep Creek Lake: The Founders*.

The lakes disappeared when Deep Creek Lake filled up. So, in a state that has no natural lake, Maryland has stacked lakes in Garrett County.

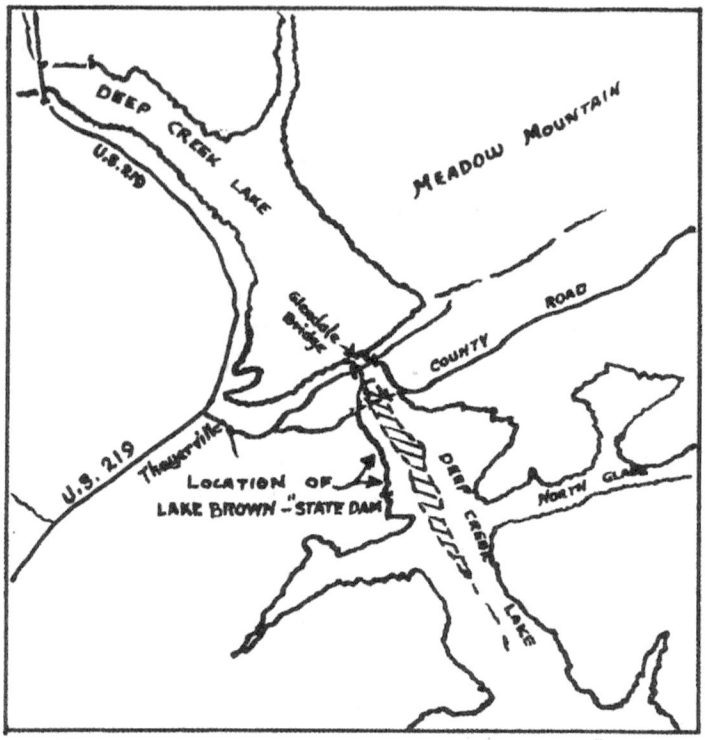

A map showing the location of Lake Brown based on an old state map. Reprinted with permission from the Garrett County Historical Society.

What Lies Beneath

L ooking at Deep Creek Lake with its wind-rippled water, one would never realize the dangers that lay below the surface.

The 3,900 acres that the lake covers were once forests and farmlands. Developers purchased 140 farms and moved 52 buildings to get ready to fill the low areas.

Frank R. Corliss was the surveyor in charge of mapping the lake bottom. "He did the surveys of the lake bottom marking where the land was to be cleared and setting the Yough concrete monuments still being used today," Ed King wrote in *Deep Creek Lake: The Founders*.

Part of his job involved keeping track of the tree cutting to make sure that not only would the tree line remaining be above the water line for the lake, but it should also be above the buffer line in case the Youghiogheny Hydro Electric Company decided to raise the level of the lake.

Crews were responsible for clearing the area that would form the lake bed. Brush and smaller trees were burned. However, some of the larger trees, particularly white pine, could be as much as four feet in diameter. Those trees were cut, but not all of them could be removed because the proper equipment wasn't available. Those trees were trimmed and left where they fell.

King tells the story of how Corliss and Arch Bittinger had a disagreement. Bittinger was in charge of actually removing the trees in the North Glade area before the lake started filling. At the time, the area had another lake near the present

Glendale Bridge that was impounded by a state dam. The lake wasn't small, but Corliss told Bittinger that when the new lake filled, the dam would be under 30 feet of water.

Bittinger couldn't believe it and thought that more trees were being removed than needed to be. So he bet Corliss $5 (about $90 today) that the water in the new lake would never reach the high-water mark.

The Deep Creek Bridge on MD Route 219 as water was filling the lake. Debris that would soon be under water can be seen in the foreground. Reprinted with permission from the Garrett County Historical Society.

It took about two years to cut the trees and clear the brush, roughly as long as it took to build the dam and power plant. However, that did not end the work with the trees that had been left on the ground.

"Shortly after the lake was flooded the remaining logs began to float and would create log jams along the shoreline depending on the direction of the wind," King wrote.

A boat named *Mary Jane* was used to tow the floating logs to McHenry. There they were pulled from the water, allowed to dry, and then cut into logs.

After the lake had filled, Bittinger walked into Corliss's office and paid off his debt. The state dam was far beneath the lake's surface.

It is not the only thing beneath the surface, either. Wells from the homes that were moved disappeared beneath the water.

Also, the stumps from the trees that were cut down sat under the water. This created a time bomb of sorts in the lake. The water loosened the ground around the roots of the stump. As it saturated the ground, it loosened it, and the stumps began floating to the surface.

"To this day the large white pine stumps are still coming loose from the bottom and are drifting out into the main body of the lake," King wrote.

While it might not be a problem for a canoe or row boat, a power boat or a sail boat moving at a good clip could be damaged if it hit a floating stump.

This created a problem for some of the early boaters on the canal. In "History of the Deep Creek Yacht Club 1937-1987," John Schaidt said, "We kept our boat in a large barn near the present Will O' the Wisp and found the sport exciting, but dangerous because of partly submerged stumps and logs floating sometimes just below the surface of the newly-filled lake."

The creation of Deep Creek Lake also required the building or relocation of fifteen miles of finished roads and old bridges. One of those bridges was near the North Point Inn.

"Each week as we passed this area, we would notice how close the encroaching water was to the old state road," John Grant wrote in *The Glades Star*. "Gradually it covered the road and the bridge as it got higher and high. For a week or so, only the three-foot-high side walls of the structure could be seen; then they also disappeared under the lake's surface."

He pointed out that the paved roads weren't removed, so there were locations where roads went right into the lake. While it was bad news for cars, the submerged roads made excellent boat launches.

Somerfield, Pennsylvania

However, as far as underwater surprises go, those in the Deep Creek Lake might be more dangerous, but not as surprising as those in other nearby lakes.

The Youghiogheny River was dammed much like its tributary, Deep Creek, which formed Deep Creek Lake. However, the work of damming the Youghiogheny began in 1939 and, slowed by World War II, was completed in 1944.

Prior to this project, the riverside had been home to many communities. Somerfield, Thomasdale, Jockey Hollow, Watsondale, Guard, Mill Run, Geise, Kempton, Sloan's Ford, and part of Selbysport were thriving communities, but they would be underwater when the reservoir filled.

The towns are in Pennsylvania, and Somerfield is the closest to the Mason Dixon Line. It once sat on the National Road, which was the reason for it being founded in 1818.

"Several U.S. Presidents visited, including Zachary Taylor and Herbert Hoover," Mary Reisinger wrote in her article, "Youghiogheny River Towns Submerged." "President William McKinley spent six weeks in Somerfield each summer, staying at the Youghiogheny Hotel, because he had relatives nearby. His niece Mabel McKinley was playing in the hotel with the son of the owner when she threw a ball that went through a window above the door."

The need for a regional water source that would serve tens of thousands outweighed the needs of the few thousand people who lived in the small towns. The government bought the homes and demolished them. The river was dammed, and the reservoir filled.

A view of Somerfield, Pennsylvania, before it disappeared beneath the waters of Youghiogheny Lake.

However, during times of extreme drought, the water drains away, and visitors can walk along the old streets and sidewalks of the town. The building foundations and wells are still visible, as are some stumps from trees that once lined the streets. An old arch bridge even becomes visible. Meanwhile, higher up on the surrounding hills, floating docks lay against the hills, waiting for the water to return.

The last time this happened was in 1998-1999.

Shaw, West Virginia

To the south of Deep Creek, along the Garrett County border with West Virginia, is Jennings Randolph Lake. This is another reservoir, but this one is in West Virginia.

The U.S. Army Corps of Engineers created the lake as part of the Flood Control Act of October 23, 1962. However, the project wasn't completed until 1981, and when it was, the town of Shaw, West Virginia, was no more.

The railroad depot in Shaw, West Virginia, before it was submerged below the Jennings Randolph Lake.

The town was a trade center for farmers in the 19th century. As coal became an industry in the area, it served the mines because it sat on the railroad line and also had a depot, particularly H. P Brydon and Brothers. Then in 1934, it became a lumber town when the Potomac Lumber Company relocated there.

However, as plans were made for the construction of the Upper Potomac River in the early 1970s, the government purchased properties. People moved out. The Western Maryland Railroad was relocated. And finally, the reservoir filled, turning Shaw into a memory.

LAKE LIFE

The Odd Boats on Deep Creek Lake

G iven that the first boats on Deep Creek Lake include canoes with outriggers and a sail, is it any wonder that odd boats have traveled the lake's waters?

The swan boat

On July 1, 1964, people on and around Deep Creek Lake watched as a giant swan moved across the waters. Although designed to look like a swan, it was actually an eighteen-foot-long boat with the top of the swan's head reaching ten feet above the water. It could seat up to eight people as it carried them around the lake, driven by a forty-horse power, two-cycle engine that was housed in the tail.

"In her first year of service, 979 passengers had the pleasure of riding on Mr. Obenshain's boat, and over the next 25 years the passenger list exceeded 7,000 entries," Dan Whetzel wrote in Mountain Discoveries.

The unique boat was a creation of inventor David Noel "Obie" Obenshain, who built it after watching migrating swans inspired him.

The mouth on the swan boat would open when the boat horn blew. One eye was a green running light, and the other eye was a red running light. It had a white light on the tail. The head could also be lowered when the boat went under low bridges.

"Children were especially thrilled at the sight of Deep

Creek's swan and if their parents were lucky enough to own a boat, they could ride as an escort to become better acquainted with the friendly bird," Whetzel wrote.

Migrating swans inspired David Obenshain to build his swan boat, which became a popular site on Deep Creek Lake. Reprinted with permission from the Garrett County Historical Society.

However, swan sightings grew less frequent over the years, and by 1991, its journey ended. "The graceful bird had aged and was not feeling well. Paint was flaking and wood was creaking. Many repairs were necessary to make the craft passenger ready and her demise was inevitable," Whetzel wrote.

Obenshain donated the swan boat to a marina, hoping the owners would repair it and put it back into use. This didn't happen, and Obenshain died in 1994.

Its fate became legend as no one seemed to know what had happened to it, only that it no longer sailed the lake.

Years later, Larry and Mark Madson, of Pittsburgh,

tracked the boat down, but it was in such poor shape, it couldn't be used for sailing. Instead of restoring the original boat, a new one was built using the original boat as the pattern. While it appears the same as the original boat, the swan boat now sports a more powerful, sixty-horsepower engine.

"A new generation of children can now enjoy the same great experience as their parents had at Deep Creek Lake. Thanks to the Madson's, the swan tradition continues," Lance C. Bell wrote in Mountain Discoveries.

The ice boat

Located in the mountains of western Maryland, the winters in Garrett County can get cold. Winter temperatures range from an average high of 38°F to an average low of 20°F. The county also typically gets 50 to 100 inches of snow a year.

In the early winters after Deep Creek Lake was created, some of the old roads still existed and ran right into the water, or as the case may be, the ice when the lake froze in the winter.

"In the winter, when the ice was thick enough, a person could drive down the road and right out onto the ice," Gerald Iman wrote in *The Glades Star.*

He remembered someone from Oakland driving a Model A Ford onto the ice and watching it spin in circles on purpose. The point was residents enjoyed the ice and testing what could be done on it.

Iman said in the 1930s he and his friends decided to build an ice boat. Most of the parts were scavenged from around Oakland, but they did have to send away for an airplane propeller.

During the 1930s, a group of young men built an ice boat that would glide across Deep Creek Lake. Reprinted with permission from the Garrett County Historical Society.

The final product had a wood frame with heavy rods and turnbuckles to hold the engine. It was covered in tin with a headlight mounted on the front. The runners were wood with steel straps to travel on the ice. The engine was a four-cylinder engine scavenged from an old Chevrolet. A rudder that controlled the front of the runners provided the steering.

Iman and his friends took the boat to a spot near the Glendale Road Bridge and took their first trip across the ice. He wrote, "…even at a low speed the iceboat jolted very badly over the rough ice. It was evident that the iceboat needed some kind of a spring system."

The other flaw they discovered was that the boat needed more weight in the front so that the front runners, which steered the boat, could grip the ice and turn it when needed. As it was, the boat needed to be slowed considerably before it could be turned.

The boys ran the boat over the frozen lake for several weeks until the ice began to melt. It was then returned to a garage in Oakland with plans to make needed improvements. However, as young men do, something else captured their attention. The improvements were never made, and the ice-boat never glided across the lake again.

The boys later came up with another creation. Iman said, "The ice was there and we had to do something with it."

Inspired by barnstormers and their airplanes, which were popular at the time, the boys decided to build what they called an "ice plane." The believed if they built an airplane fuselage on skis, it would provide them a smoother ride across the ice than the ice boat.

The bought a mail-order propeller from *Popular Mechanics* and powered it with an engine from a Harley-Davidson motorcycle. What they didn't give it was wings. Although they called it an "ice plane," it was more of a hybrid between their ice boat and an airplane.

Once the lake froze thick enough, the boys hauled the ice plane to the creek and started the engine.

"Everything worked fine as long as the ice plane moved at a slow speed," Iman wrote. "However, when it went faster the tail would raise up and it would swing around into the wind like a weather vane. No matter what we did, it would slew around into the wind."

With their second effort falling short of expectations, the boys stored their creations in an Oakland garage. However, ice boating still continues on the lake, although the boats nowadays are professionally constructed and are essentially sailboats on sleds.

Greg Shafer enjoys sailing across a frozen Deep Creek Lake. Photo courtesy of Cheryl Shafer with the Deep Creek Lake Sailing Association.

The Turkey Neck Queen

The 1951 movie, The African Queen, starring Humphrey Bogart and Katharine Hepburn is considered a classic. Not only did it win Bogart an Academy Award for Best Actor, the movie was selected for preservation in the United States National Film Registry in 1994.

However, one character in the movie that doesn't get much recognition is the boat that gave the movie its name, *The African Queen*. It was a small steamboat that served as the setting for much of the movie.

Garrett County businessman Charles McIntire and lawyer Bernard Fensterwald were friends who both shared a love of steam engines and wooden boats.

"We were both fond of wooden boats and decided we

needed something exciting to do. At the time there was a company in New England that sold steam boats, so we made a decision to purchase one. But unlike other customers who bought the boat fully assembled, Bernard and I decided that we wanted to build it ourselves. We were optimists. Of course we knew about *The African Queen* but it was mostly an interest in boats that motivated us to buy it," McIntire said in an article in Mountain Discoveries.

They chose to rebuild the movie boat on a smaller scaler, but their version still had a scaled-down wood-burning boiler that provided a half horsepower. The boat could also seat four people.

Although it was initially a passion project for the two men, because progress was so slow, they had to get outside help to bring it to completion. At the Deep Creek Yacht Club, it was christened *The Turkey Neck Queen,* in honor of both the movie and where the yacht club was located on Deep Creek Lake.

"The *Turkey Neck Queen* proved to be a slow but steady craft that drew attention. The distinctive ker-chunk, ker-chunk, ker-chunk sound accompanied by puffs of steam provided an anachronistic vision to onlookers," Whetzel wrote in Mountain Discoveries.

The boat also had a distinctive whistle, which doubled as a way to reduce boiler pressure.

McIntire and Fensterwald traveled around the lake primarily in the Rock Lodge area for several years in the 1970s before retiring the boat. It can now be seen on display in the Garrett County Museum of Transportation.

The Turkey Neck Queen is a smaller version of *The African Queen*, featured in the movie by the same name. Photo from the author's collection.

The Lake Births a Park

A lthough not planned as a recreation and tourism draw for Garrett County, Deep Creek Lake was an immediate success not only in those areas but in its planned purpose to generate power at the Deep Creek Hydroelectric Station.

Planning for a large lake as a source for hydroelectric power began as early as 1908, but early attempts to create such a lake fell through. It wasn't until 1921 that a viable plan took shape. The idea was to build four dams and three powerhouses.

Even this plan would change as it moved from concept to land acquisition and construction in November 1923. Around 8,000 acres (including 140 farms) were purchased, although only 4,500 acres would be underwater. The excess land was used to create a buffer strip around the edge of the lake to allow for the water level to rise if needed without encroaching on private property.

Charles Hawley & Company of Washington, D.C. built the first dam and powerhouse at the confluence of Deep Creek and the Yough River, employing 1,000 men in the construction. Besides the actual construction of a dam and powerhouse, a connection needed to be built to the B&O Railroad in Oakland, 15 miles of road needed to be relocated, two steel bridges needed to be relocated, and a stone quarry needed to be opened and operated.

The power plant opened on May 26, 1925. The dam is 1,340 feet wide across Deep Creek and is located about 1.75

miles upstream from the river's confluence with the Yough River. The powerhouse can produce 18 megawatts of power.

While the power generation benefitted Pennsylvania residents, local residents had watched the creation of the lake. In the summer the waters beckoned to boaters, swimmers, and fishermen. In the winter, the frozen lake called to skaters and ice boats. Deep Creek Lake is Maryland's largest freshwater lake. It covers 3,900 acres and has 65 miles of shoreline.

A few months after the power plant went online, the Youghiogheny Hydroelectric Company granted the State of Maryland control of the buffer.

It was about a year after the power plant opened that officials started thinking about creating a park along the shoreline of the lake. Conservation Commissioner of Maryland Swepson Earle was one of the early advocates for a state park. He told a group of Garrett County businessmen that he wasn't authorized to speak for the governor, but he felt Gov. Albert Ritchie would support "any move that tended to the health and happiness of the people of the State and that he would promise his support," the *Cumberland Sunday Times* reported in 1926.

However, the park wouldn't become a reality for many years.

In the meantime, private entrepreneurs started developing the lake's commercial potential. Cabins appeared along the shoreline to house visitors to the county for even longer stretches of time as Garrett County found itself a tourist destination.

Finally, in 1956, the State of Maryland began planning for a state park along the lake. The project took three years to come to fruition as the State Department of Forests and Parks received partial appropriations from the General Assembly that allowed the park work to move forward slowly.

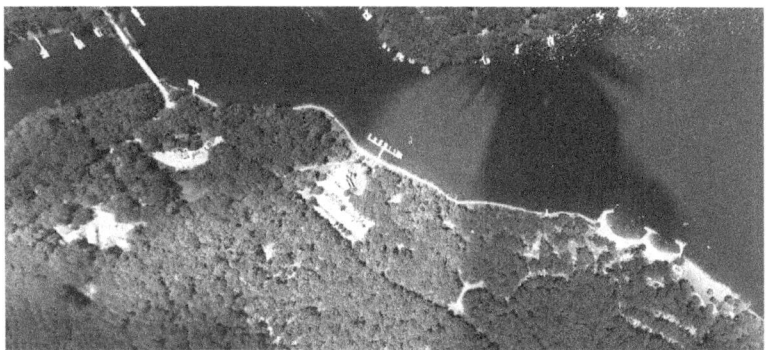

In this aerial view of Deep Creek Lake State Park, you can see the beach area on the right (looks like a W) and the boat docks near the Discovery Center in the center of the picture. Photo courtesy of Instantstreetview.com.

Deep Creek Lake State Park opened on July 1, 1959. It employed seven maintenance men and two lifeguards. It was an immediate success, so much so that the state was already looking to expand the park the following year.

"The park, at one time a game refuge, officially opened July 1 of this year and has been accommodating an average of 2,500 to 3,000 persons on Sunday," the *Cumberland News* reported.

The recreation area of the park had a mile of shoreline along the lake (800 feet of which were beach) and was made up of 150 acres of a 1764-acre layout. The campground could house fifty-five families. Campers could stay for $7 a week or $1.25 a night.

There was also a bathhouse, laundry facilities, 154 picnic tables and fireplaces, and restrooms in the picnic area. There were seven parking sections with two landings for each parking section. Parking was fifty cents on weekends and holidays.

"Catering to patrons from the Cumberland area and the Baltimore-Washington area, in addition to the many Pennsylvania users, the park is practically filled during open hours, particularly the camping sites," the *Cumberland News* reported.

Today, the park has over 1,800 acres. "With its mile long shore line, two swimming beaches, 20 miles of hiking/biking trails, 112 site campground, and 6,000 square foot Discovery Center, Deep Creek Lake State Park offers year round activities for everyone," according to the park's website.

Racing Across the Water

Would it surprise you to know that Deep Creek Lake has not just one yacht club, but two?

Of course, it all depends on what you consider a yacht.

By strict definition, a sailboat might be considered a yacht. It's a private sailing vessel used for non-commercial purposes, including sailing.

However, most people don't think of a sailboat when they hear the word yacht. Although there are no strict standards, yachts are generally larger, with more amenities, require more maintenance, and cost more than boats. Boats are used more for recreational activities such as fishing and water skiing, whereas yachts are used more for leisure and cruising.

Deep Creek Lake has had its own yacht club since 1937, although those first yachts were rowboats and canoes, according to the Garrett County Museum of Transportation. The first sailboat on the lake appeared in 1926. John Schaidt built it by adding a sail to a rowboat, according to John Grant in "History of the Deep Creek Yacht Club 1937-1987." Canoes had lee boards added to them to give them stability when a sail was added. The mast and boom for the sails were often made from bamboo.

"We kept our boat in a large barn near the present Will-o'-the-wisp and found the sport exciting, but dangerous because of partly submerged stumps and logs floating sometimes just below the surface of the newly filled lake," Schaidt told Grant.

Carlos Mirick had the first genuine sailboat on the lake. Grant doesn't note the year it appeared, but in context, it seems to have been the late 1920s.

As vacationing at Deep Creek Lake grew in popularity, more boats appeared. Other sailboats were built, and soon, people were racing each other.

"Father sold land to Gordon Sprague from Washington. They built a sailboat on the same plan as ours, and we would race and chase all over the lake." Alice Mirick, Carlos Mirick's daughter, told Grant.

A shot from the 2013 Laser Regatta on Deep Creek Lake. Photo courtesy of Cheryl Shafer with the Deep Creek Lake Sailing Association.

John Mordock brought the first manufactured boat to the lake in 1934, a Bell Class Swallow with a 15.5-foot keel. He had moved to Cumberland from Chicago where he had been a member of the yacht club and wanted something similar in Garrett County.

A group of boaters, which would form the core of the Deep Creek Yacht Club, used to meet at the Will 'O the Wisp, where they would set out for days of boating and racing on the lake.

"One Sunday afternoon we were approached by a short man wearing leather boots and a wide-brimmed hat," Schaidt said. "He said his name was Harry Muma, and that he and a partner, Cy Bowers, had just bought a piece of land south of the Glendale Bridge. He called it Turkey Neck and said if we would bring our group and boats down and sail off his property that he would build us a Yacht Club."

It was an offer the group couldn't pass up, so Nancy James, Susan Farris, John Murrie, John Mordock, and John Schaidt, all from Cumberland; Tau Rowe from Westernport; and Dick Holben from Frostburg sailed south and went under the Glendale Bridge and continued onto Turkey Neck.

"We all gathered in the foundation; Muma cracked a bottle of Gilbey's gin and said, 'This will be your Yacht Club,'" Schaidt said.

Muma said it would take a year to build a proper clubhouse, so Mordock purchased a lot where the group could put a temporary one. A log cabin arrived the following week on a truck from Sears-Roebuck. For the next two weeks, the group constructed the cabin, dug a well, put in a septic system, and built an entrance to the club and a dock.

The club was dedicated in the spring of 1937, and in June, the articles of incorporation for the Deep Creek Yacht Club were filed. The articles laid out the club goal, which is "To promote the development and use of small boats and small boat racing on Deep Creek Lake in Garrett County, Maryland, and to provide facilities therefore."

With the creation of the yacht club, Mordock became the first commodore.

The Deep Creek Yacht Club clubhouse before its 2024 renovations. Photo courtesy of Cheryl Shafer with the Deep Creek Lake Sailing Association.

When the permanent clubhouse opened, it became the center of activity for members. It featured dormitories, a kitchen, and a large dining room.

The yacht club became a draw for the area and attracted plenty of people to buy up nearby lakefront lots. The racing results also started appearing in newspapers from Pittsburgh to Baltimore and Washington, D.C.

By the 1960s, the yacht club had grown in popularity so much that the facilities were strained to accommodate everyone. There was also a dispute over how the clubhouse should be used.

"When conflicts arose over use of the building in the mid 60's, the local sailors led by Don Hott, John Schaidt, Fred Steiding, Howard Buchanan, and Ken Farrell designed and built their own facility on Thousand Acres and became the Deep Creek Yacht Club at Deer Haven," Joan B. Crawford wrote in "Deep Creek Yacht Club at Turkey Neck."

That club is now called the Deep Creek Yacht Club, and

the Deep Creek Yacht Club at Turkey Neck is incorporated at the Deep Creek Sailing Association.

Both clubs continue to thrive and provide a social network for regular visitors to lake.

The yacht clubs run races and events throughout the summer, generally late April until the end of September. Racing runs from Memorial Day to Labor Day. You can also see annual regattas on the lake if you are there at the right time.

Boaters sailing on Deep Creek Lake. Photo courtesy of Cheryl Shafer with the Deep Creek Lake Sailing Association.

Ski Trains to McHenry

W
hen the Wisp Ski Resort first opened in the mid-1950s, it was a half-day trip to drive from Washington, D. C. or Baltimore to McHenry. This was in the days before Interstate 68 opened, so visitors traveled through Western Maryland along Route 40 before heading south on Route 219.

It wasn't long before the Baltimore and Ohio Railroad decided to offer "ski trains" to the resort. The problem was that the nearest railroad to McHenry was in Oakland, fourteen miles away.

McHenry did have a railroad at one time. When Deep Creek Lake was being constructed, a narrow-gauge railroad had been built. All the needed building materials—gravel, rock, sand, concrete, steel, and lumber—needed to be brought into the area to build the dam and roads that were needed. Those tracks ran from the Oakland train station to the dam, the power plant, and the stone quarry in McHenry.

"In all, 12 miles of standard gauge track were constructed including temporary bridges and trestles," Ed King wrote on *Deep Creek Lake: The Founders.*

The narrow-gauge railroad would have been perfect to bring in skiers and lake vacationers to the area. Unfortunately, by the time the Wisp Ski Resort opened, those tracks had been removed.

However, in December 1957, the *Oakland Republican* announced that the B&O Railroad was going to be offering ski excursion rates that season on The National Limited.

The old Baltimore and Ohio Railroad train station in Oakland. Built in 1883, it served as a train station until 1981. Courtesy of Wikimedia Commons.

The National Limited was an all-Pullman car train that traveled between Jersey City, New Jersey and St. Louis, Missouri on the B&O Railroad. It was the first long-distance train to be entirely air-conditioned.

Passengers on the train could enjoy a twelve-ounce sirloin steak with a salad, potato, bread, and a beverage for just $4.75 (about $52 in 2023 dollars). Other dinners included bacon-wrapped steak, Chesapeake oysters, fish, and chicken. You could also order less-expensive items a la carte. Alcoholic drinks could be purchased for 85 cents (about $9 in 2023 dollars).

The train left Baltimore, Washington D.C., and Silver Spring, Maryland, on Friday mornings and traveled to Oakland. From there, buses carried the skiers to a hotel near the ski resort. They could then spend all day Saturday on the slopes, spend a second night in the hotel, ski on Sunday for a half day, and then return east by bus and train.

The cost for two days of skiing, two nights of accommodations in the hotel, and all transportation was $24 (about $260 in 2023 dollars).

Two years later, the newspaper reported, "These trips are reportedly a lot of fun and recapture the atmosphere of the ski trains of yesteryear when half the fun was getting there."

Swanton Shootout Leads to Congressional Recognition

J oe Friend ran a small store in Swanton, Maryland, in the early twentieth century. He also served as the postmaster, and the post office was part of his store. Although he owned a home nearby where his family live, Joe often slept in the store.

"But Joe Friend took his responsibility to heart and guarded the U.S. Mail and the store contents by sleeping in a room adjoining the main room used for merchandise and the post office area that was partitioned from the public," according to *The Glades Star*.

He was sleeping in the store on September 25, 1925, with a .38-caliber pistol and flashlight on the nightstand beside the bed. The store was beside the Baltimore and Ohio Railroad tracks, and the noise of passing trains often filled the store. It was an expected noise, though, and it didn't disturb Joe's sleep.

The noise that woke him was softer, but out of place. Joe woke up and listened, trying to place the sound that had awakened him.

He had heard someone moving around in the post office area.

He stood up in his long underwear and picked up his pistol and flashlight. He quietly moved to the door of the storeroom and then turned on the flashlight.

"Death flashed at him with the roar of a gunshot and

missed Joe by only a hair. A terrific blow struck the left side of his head," according *The Glades Star.* "He staggered against the door jamb, but he did not go down."

Even as he dropped his flashlight, he shot back in the direction of the muzzle flash. Joe heard someone grunt in pain, and then a weight—he assumed it was a body, —slammed against the partition that separated the post office from the store area.

Joseph Fletcher Friend, II. Reprinted with permission from the Garrett County Historical Society.

With blood running down his face, Joe jumped over the store counter. The thief shot at him again, and Joe fired back.

The thief retreated into the mail storage area. Joe ran over to the door and started firing into it. The thief fired, and Joe felt something burn across his scalp.

His pistol clicked on an empty chamber, but the thief had also stopped firing. Joe dropped his pistol and rushed at the man.

They fell to the floor, punching at each other, trying to get the upper hand. Joe was a big man. He stood six feet tall and weighed 185 pounds, but he was not a young man. He was fifty-six years old, and he was wounded.

Slowly, the thief gained the upper hand, and then he began pistol whipping Joe on his head. Knowing he couldn't win, Joe stopped struggling and pretended to be unconscious.

The Swanton Post Office in 1925. Reprinted with permission from the Garrett County Historical Society.

The thief stood up and staggered out of the building.

In pain, Joe pulled himself up and followed the thief outside. He screamed for help.

Perhaps already on his way to the store drawn by the

shots, B&O Railroad Agent Wade Lohr ran across the tracks, calling Joe's name. He saw Joe was injured and helped him to his house. Then Wade went back to the train station to call County Sheriff Guy Yutzy in Oakland. He also alerted the telegraphers along the railroad.

Sheriff Yutzy arrived by car within an hour, and he brought Dr. N. I. Broadwater with him. While the doctor examined Joe, the sheriff organized a posse among the people who were gathering at the home. Word had spread quickly through the area, and it was believed that there had been more than one thief.

Dr. Broadwater saw Joe's wounds were serious. He gave Joe a painkiller and dressed his wounds. "He knew that either wound could have brought instant death if it had varied slightly," *The Glades Star* reported. "He found that the pistol clubbing had broken the lower jawbone and suspected Joe's upper face and bones were fractured also."

The doctor had Wade ask the train dispatcher to have the eastbound No. 2 train stop at Swanton and pick up Joe.

They were still waiting for the train when the sheriff returned with a prisoner. The posse had found a large wounded man among railroad ties not far from the store. He refused to answer any questions, and no one knew who he was.

The doctor examined the man and found he had been shot in the abdomen and head. Alarmingly, he found no evidence that the bullet had exited the man's head.

The train arrived, Joe was loaded onto it, and it left Swanton around midnight. Only two hours had passed since Joe had been awakened in the store.

The prisoner was initially taken back to Oakland, but then because of the severity of the prisoner's wounds and the fact that he had committed a federal crime trying to rob a post office, Sheriff Yutzy transferred the man to Cumberland to await trial.

B&O Railroad police officers caught Ralph Anderson two days later near Grafton, West Virginia. He had been identified as the second thief that at the store, but he had run off when the shooting started.

He admitted to police that he had only met his accomplice, who was named Henderson Hall, that day. Henderson was making his way across the country, but he was down on his luck and needed money. They had gotten to talking and decided to rob the store. Ralph served as the lookout until things went bad.

When police ran Henderson's name, they discovered he was a Jamaican sailor, who was wanted in Baltimore.

Joe was treated at Western Maryland Hospital. Sadly, he lost his left eye as a result of his injuries.

For all Joe's suffering, Henderson Hall was doing worse. He had been taken from Oakland to the Western Maryland Hospital in Cumberland. He underwent two surgeries, one for the bullet wound in his abdomen, but the other was a trepanning of his skull. This is an outdated form of brain surgery that involved removing pieces of the skull.

"A portion of the brain was removed and it is said the surgeons could not locate the bullet," according to the *Cumberland Evening Times.*

He was given a hearing in the hospital and held for the federal courts under heavy guard, even though he was no threat. He remained in the hospital, recovering for a month before he was taken to the county jail.

In the interim, Ralph Anderson had been taken to Baltimore for his trial, where he was found guilty and sentenced to prison.

Although Henderson wasn't in danger of dying, he was paralyzed and, like Joe, had lost an eye. He also could not speak. Most of this was due to one of Joe's shots hitting him in the brain.

"His plight is the most tragic of any prisoner ever confined in the county prison," the Cumberland Evening Times reported. "Sometimes Hall in his helplessness will slump over and slide from his cot to his knees on his cell floor with face and body bowed over as if imploring Heaven to relieve him of his distressing existence."

It was said that the jail guards and other prisoners took pity on him and treated him kindly. They fed and bathed him, but most of the time, he lay in his cot "like the phantom of a human being existing between the borderland of life and death.

His condition kept him from ever being tried for the crime of robbing a post office, but he never regained his health and remained hospitalized.

In June 1928, the U.S. government recognized Joe's bravery and authorized the payment of $2,000 (about $35,000 in 2024 dollars) as a reward for the capture and arrest of Henderson. The Republican noted, "Mr. Friend could not receive the customary reward offered by the Postoffice Department because of the fact that Hall was never convicted of the crime which he committed."

This meant that a bill had to be passed by both the U.S. House of Representatives and U.S. Senate and signed by President Calvin Coolidge in order for Joe to receive any money.

Joe never fully regained his health, and he died in 1930 at age 61. He is buried in the George Cemetery in Swanton.

Maryland Buys a Lake

W ith the creation of Deep Creek Lake, Garrett County had a large natural resource that residents, and soon, tourists, wanted to use. The Youghiogheny Hydroelectric Company owned the lake and the property that bordered it. Technically, to get to the lake, you had to trespass on private property.

Not that the company was too concerned as long as water flowed through the turbines, generating electricity.

So, the State of Maryland stepped in to help, recognizing the lake's value as a natural resource. At the end of July 1925, two months after the power plant went live, the Maryland State Conservation Commissioner Swepson Earle said that the Youghiogheny Hydroelectric Company had "turned over" Deep Creek Lake.

This actually meant that the company had given Maryland the right to manage the lake and the buffer strip.

"Mr. Earle also said it is proposed to make Deep Creek Lake a trout lake which will draw fishermen from all over Western Maryland and other States to its shores," the *Oakland Republican* reported. "The transfer of 12,000 rainbow and brook trout from the Lewistown hatchery to the pool will begin immediately."

This was an arrangement that worked well enough for everyone. It allowed Maryland to create a new state park, residents and tourists to enjoy water activities, the county's economy to flourish, and the Youghiogheny Hydroelectric Company to get power and usage fees from the lake.

Over the years, though, other companies bought the Youghiogheny Hydroelectric Company and some of them had differing ideas about what to do with Deep Creek Lake. And, of course, the State of Maryland was anxious to actually own the largest lake in the state, even if it was man-made.

A peaceful afternoon on Deep Creek Lake. Photo from the author's collection.

In 1995, a group of lake property owners floated the idea of buying the lake because they weren't sure what the future would hold with either owner. "Ever since the lake fell under a five-year management agreement between Maryland's Department of Natural Resources and the utility, lake users became worried about long-term lake access," the *Garrett County Weekender* reported.

Although the idea didn't gain any traction, a company spokesman said at a public meeting the following year, "we have no intention of selling the lake." However, two years later, GPU, the company that owned the lake, announced it was for sale.

In January 2000, it was announced that the State of Maryland had agreed to purchase the lake property and buffer strip amounting to roughly 5,000 acres, the power plant, and the dam for $17.6 million, roughly twice what the original lake, dam, and powerhouse cost.

Business and property owners around the lake were happy because the agreement kept the operation of the lake status quo and maintained property owners' rights.

With the purchase of Deep Creek Lake, it became part of Maryland's park system.

John Nelson, Garrett County Planning and Zoning Director, said the state will own the land up to the high water mark that was 2,466 foot in elevation. "There will still be a circumference around the entire lake, from the actual edge of the water, that people can walk across or fish from," he said. Everything above that line was offered to the adjoining landowners.

Getting Closer to God

S ome people feel enjoying time on the lake allows them to grow closer to God. Certainly the Congregation of the Holy Cross of Washington, D.C., and Discalced Carmelite Friars of the Washington Province of Carmelite in Washington D.C. felt that way.

Beginning in 1927, the Congregation of the Holy Cross had started renting property from the Browning Family near the Narrows Bridge to provide a summer camp for the seminarians in Washington to give them a chance to get away from their studies and the heat of the city.

In 1930, they decided they wanted their own property with permanent structures, and they approached the Pennsylvania Electric Power Corporation about selling property to the Congregation of the Holy Cross.

"The power company proved to be reluctant about the sale because it didn't desire to become embroiled in real estate development issues," Dan Whetzel wrote in *Mountain Discoveries.*

Luckily, the Lohr family had decided they wanted to move from their property along the lake.

"The land originally belonged to the Lohr family prior to the lake's construction, and according to Father Melody, Mrs. Lohr wanted to move from the homestead, as she believed the rising waters near the house threatened the safety of her children," Whetzel wrote.

The Congregation of the Holy Cross wound up purchasing the thirty-six acres of the Lohr property that weren't underwater for $3,000 (about $56,000 in 2024 dollars).

With a permanent camp of their own, the seminarians began adding to it. The seminarians lived in tents on the property until the lodge was completed in 1932. The dining hall was completed in 1932. The chapel was built in 1937. A modern addition to the property was a 9-hole, par-36 golf course.

The seminarians would leave Washington D.C. for camp in mid-June each year. "Oftentimes, they arranged for an extra railcar to be added to the train, and they 'sang and had a picnic all the way to Cumberland,'" John R. Paige wrote in "Holy Cross Camp of Deer Park, Maryland, The Foundation Years: 1930-1945."

They transferred trains at Cumberland to one that stopped at Oakland on its way to St. Louis. Two local families with trucks met them at the Oakland train station and drove the seminarians out to the Deep Creek Lake camp.

In the early days, the seminarians wore uniforms while at the camp. This was khaki shirts and pants, army shoes, and a white sailor's hat–all purchased from an Army/Navy surplus store in Washington. The hat apparently helped distinguish the seminarians from revenue agents.

Paige quoted one of the priests from the camp who told a story of when a group of the seminarians got stuck on a mountain in an old Model T truck. "Some gunmen came out of the woods and asked us who we were and what we were doing. I explained and they opened up the truck to examine the contents, see what we had. Because we had khaki clothes on, they were suspicious of us. After we had satisfied their curiosity they insisted we take a drink, moonshine. We refused for our stomach's sake and then they wanted to give us money. We took it because it would be wise to take it and not irritate them. They let us go then. Later on, we heard that another party had blundered into their camp and were killed."

Most days followed a routine of getting up at 6 a.m., having morning prayers and meditation, then morning Mass, followed by breakfast. Afterwards, there would be chores to do and time for quiet reading. However, between prayers and lunch at noon and prayers and dinner at 6 p.m., the afternoon was free.

"Not all activities were religious. The priests and brothers of the Holy Cross formed a baseball team. The Holy Cross team would travel to Oakland, Deer Park, Crellin, Terra Alta, Westernport, Morgantown, and Kitzmiller. Their travel accommodations were the back of an old pick-up truck. In return for the spirited baseball games and competitions, the priest would host their opposing teams at the retreat as their guests," according to a plaque at the Garrett County Museum of Transportation.

After decades of service to the church, the compound was sold in 2003 for $77.7 million.

On the other side of the lake from the Holy Cross summer camp was a huge home that was once called the Mount Carmel Monastery of the Discalced Carmelite Friars.

The Congregation of Holy Cross had been at Deep Creek Lake for fifteen years when Father Thomas Kilduff with the Discalced Carmelite Friars of the Washington Province of Carmelite in Washington D.C. bought fifty-three acres at Deep Creek Lake for $3,000 (about $52,000 in 2024 dollars) so that the friars could escape the stifling city heat in the summer.

Unlike the Holy Cross seminarians, the Carmelite friars are a contemplative order. They spend much of the day in prayer, going barefoot or wearing sandals (This is what discalced means.).

A building was constructed on the property that the Carmelites named Mount Carmel after the mountain in Israel, where the order began in the twelfth century. It began as a small, one-story building with ten small "cells," which are the rooms where the friars stayed. There was also a community room, kitchen, and community bathroom. It had no fireplaces or heating, which they didn't believe was needed since they were only there during the summer. If the weather did happen to get cold, the friars closed the wooden shutters on the windows. About 100 yards from the monastery was a fasting shed where the monks could go to spend days praying while they went without food.

The Mount Carmel Monastery of the Discalced Carmelite Friars was a summer retreat for the friars.

According to the website for the former Deep Creek Lake monastery, "The entire student Carmelite community, accompanied by the older Friars, and nuns from the Carmelite Sisters of Baltimore, were transferred to Deep Creek Lake each spring to continue their Carmelite life, until time to return to Washington in the fall."

Besides fasting, the monks also kept an odd-looking boat

at the monastery to allow them to sail about the lake.

"There was an old lady named Mrs. Smith who lived in a house up by the Glendale bridge and the monks used to take the boat up to visit her, and she would feed them pie," according to the website.

Over the years, additional rooms were added and older rooms were enlarged. The monks did all the work themselves, with the exception of the concrete block walls. For this, they had a church raising and had friends of the Carmelites lend their talents and labor.

Then things changed.

"With the advent of Vatican II in 1965 came the Decree of Optatam Totius which changed theological education for young priests and monks," according to the website. "The tradition of sequestering students in pastoral settings, such as Mount Carmel, gave way to studies in more urban settings at large universities and theological seminaries. The young monks were granted far more choice in their priestly training, and Mount Carmel at Deep Creek Lake fell into disuse."

Older Carmelites still visited, but with the death of Father Kilduff in 1989, the decision was made to sell the property. The property was subdivided into smaller lots, and the monastery is now rented to vacationers as the Inn at Carmel Cove.

NEAR THE LAKE

The Airport Beneath the Highway

I n the late 1960s, the McHenry section of U.S. Highway 219 was realigned and widened. The S. J. Groves Company was hired to move the highway off of its Deep Creek Drive alignment to its current location.

One day, Charles "Skeeter" Bowman met the workers at the edge of his property and had them halt construction.

"They had these giant bulldozers and scrapers ready to cut through my grass airstrip, and I made them stop while I taxied out and took off one last time," Bowman told the *Cumberland Times News* in 1999.

It may also have been the last flight out of the Garrett County's first airfield.

Bowman was a lifelong resident of Garrett County and a veteran of WWII where he served as an aerial gunner on a B-29 bomber, based on the Pacific island of Tinian. "The B-29 crews based on Tinian flew bombing missions over Japan, with just enough gasoline to complete the two-way trip," Bowman's obituary noted in 2014. He left the service as a staff sergeant who had earned the Distinguished Flying Cross, Air Medal, Asiatic-Pacific Medal and World War II Victory Medal.

After he returned home, the Bowman family decided to covert a section of the family's dairy farm into a landing strip.

"My father gave them permission because it was the only

convenient place for aircraft to land near Deep Creek Lake," Bowman is quoted on the plaque as saying. "A majority of the pilots that landed on our farm were from the Pittsburgh area."

The airfield primarily serviced single-engine aircraft, although it also had a Piper Cub and a BT-13 (a WWII Army Air Corps trainer) land there.

"Two other unusual aircraft cruising there were designed for agricultural purposes," according to a historical display in Bear Creek Traders store in McHenry. "They arrived from the eastern shore of Maryland outfitted with sprayers that would emit a mist of insecticide. Farmers requested the service to combat aphids that were harming the local pea crop."

The Bowman family actively farmed the ninety-seven-acre property until 1946, according to the historical display.

However, it is uncertain when the airfield began operating. According to the plaque, "Bowman Airfield was not yet depicted on a 1946 aerial photo, nor on the 1949 USGS topo map." According to the website Abandoned and Little Known Airfields, the earliest appearance of Bowman Airfield on aeronautical charts was on July 1954 Huntington Sectional Chart, although the airfield was in use before then.

It was located between Mosser Road and the current U.S. 219. It was a 2,300-foot-long grass runway. Bowman made the orange windsock that flew at the airfield and let pilots know the direction the wind was blowing.

Although there was no charge to land at the airfield, services were limited. Pilots would tie down their planes next to the landing strip. Fuel was stored on the airfield in a fifty-five-gallon drum. Pilots could purchase fuel for their planes.

"We saw it as a means of recreation. We never saw it as a way to make money," Bowman said.

The field had no lights, which made night landings next to impossible.

A view of Garrett County's first airfield.

"If you wanted to land at night, you'd have someone park their cars with the headlights on along the field edge," Bowman told the *Cumberland Times News*. "You let down slowly and looked for the dim reflection of the plane's red and green position lights on the grass,"

Even with car headlights illuminating the field, it was still tricky, and few pilots willing to attempt it. This is because the surrounding mountains made the initial approach quite difficult and requiring precise landing patterns. Marsh Hill is to the west and Negro Mountain is off to the south and east.

Take-offs could be just as tricky.

"The east end of the runway was 100 feet higher than the west end, which meant takeoffs were to the west (downhill) and landings were to the east (uphill)," said Bowman.

He told the *Cumberland Times News* that he saw several pilots whose planes went nose over on a downhill landing or failed to get airborne on an uphill take-off.

Bowman used the airfield more than anyone, and he was familiar with its quirks. However, in January 1955, he chose to land his plane on the frozen Deep Creek Lake.

"I know the ice was thick enough because I went out with an ax and chopped a 2-foot-deep hole in the ice first," he said.

As the popularity of Deep Creek Lake increased, some tourists decided to fly to McHenry for vacation. Some pilots just used it as a place to stop, rest, and refuel. Businessmen used the airfield to fly to other locations and even transport some goods. One of those businessmen was Bowman himself, who had opened Bowman's Marina on the lake.

"I used to joke that I had the first airfreight service in the area because I would fly to Baltimore and pick up boating supplies and stack them in my plane," he told *Mountain Discoveries* magazine.

Because of the airfield's popularity, a forty-foot by sixty-foot hanger was built in 1954 to store Bowman's private plane. It was also used to store boats from the nearby Bowman's Marina.

Bowman said that on busy weekends, as many as eight planes would use the landing field. Although the plaque notes, "A flying club from Somerset PA also chose the field for a fly-in event, thereby temporarily creating a busy flight schedule at McHenry."

It is thought the airfield closed sometime in 1960, according to Abandoned and Little-Known Airfields. This is because the airfield is on the 1960 Huntington Sectional Chart but not the 1961 one. The confusion comes from the airfield still appearing on the 1962 USGS topo map. WVNews.com puts the end time later, reporting that flights from the airfield ended on June 25, 1969.

Little remains of the airfield. It is either under U.S. 219 or part of the Garrett County Fairgrounds. Abandoned and Little-Known Airfields quotes Bowman's daughter, Linda

Bowman Niederberger, saying, "The grass parking area of the Garrett County Fairgrounds [the eastern portion of the former airfield] is all that is left of the landing strip. The hangar is stranded on the other side of Route 219. The hangar is between the 2 roads [Route 219 and Deep Creek Drive], more or less surrounded by other structures."

Bear Creek Traders purchased Bowman's 1940 Taylorcraft BC65 plane. The 784-pound plane hangs from cables in the store as part of the historical display.

Skeeter Bowman's airplane that he used to fly from his airfield in McHenry on display in Bear Creek Traders in McHenry, Maryland.

Also, although Bowman Airfield is gone, Garrett County still has an airport. The Garrett County Airport opened about a mile north of the airfield when it closed. The airport, which the county owns, has been updated a number of times since it opened.

It has also come a long way since its grass airstrip day.

It now has a 5,000-foot runway with night lights and a parallel taxiway. The terminal has amenities for both passengers and pilots, including a snack area, offices, and meeting rooms.

Dozens of aircraft are kept them in two hangars or tied down on the field.

Cursed Land Near Deep Creek Lake

I n Garrett County, somewhere around Swallow Falls or McHenry, there is a plot of land that may be "cursed".

Early in the nineteenth century, Joseph Friend, who was a son-in-law of the Western Maryland frontiersman Meshach Browning, built a home midway between Sang Run and Oakland. In 1823, Friend had married Rachael Browning, who was the second of 11 children born to Meshach Browning and his first wife Mary McMullen.

Meshach Browning has been called Maryland's most-famous frontier hunter. He also explored much of Western Maryland. He remains well known today because of his memoir *Forty-Four Years of the Life of a Hunter*, which was first published in 1859.

Browning's father, Joshua, was an English soldier who survived Braddock's massacre in 1755. He deserted the army and settled in Western Maryland to make his way as a woodsman.

Meshach Browning learned these skills growing up. He was drafted into the military as a sergeant and served for a short time in the War of 1812. After the war, he returned home to hunt and explore. Browning estimated in his book that during his lifetime he killed "from 1800 to 2000 deer, from 300 to 400 bears, and about 50 panthers and cata-mounts, with scores of wolves and wildcats."

Friend's home, in what would eventually become Garrett County, was his dream home for his family until it burned down, killing two of Friend's sons.

The Evening Times lists the two children who died as John, 8, and Freeman, 10. However, a family tree compiled by a branch of the family indicates that Joseph Friend and Rachael Browning had ten children, but only two of them died in the same year. Mahlon and John both died in 1839. These two boys were also two years apart for a portion of the year while Freeman and John were nine years apart.

"Mr. Friend, thinking that the occurrence was one of those awful accidents that sometimes happens, rebuilt, but when his house burned down the second time in the same mysterious way that it did the first, he thought it was very strange and refused to rebuild and moved elsewhere," the newspaper reported.

Friend sold the property to a man whose last name was Bray. He knew about the mysterious fires that had burned down two homes. Undeterred, Bray built his home on the old foundation only to have it burn down a short time later.

Bray wasn't ready to give up. "Mr. Bray, like Mr. Friend, concluded that he would not rebuild on the old site or foundation, so he changed the location and had his new house erected near the old foundation," *The Evening Times* reported.

In 1899, Bray's second home burned down. The fire from the house also jumped to large barn that stood a few yards away from the house.

"Mr. Bray, like the former owner, also concludes that the spot is doomed, and will not again replace the buildings. He is terribly worried about the matter as all he has is wrapped up in his little farm," the newspaper reported.

Rachael Friend died in 1869 in Deer Park and Joseph died in 1894 in Sang Run.

The unknown plot of cursed land remains waiting for the next home to be built upon it.

A Step Back into Prehistory

W hile thousands of visitors flock to Garrett County each year to enjoy the modern marvel that is Deep Creek Lake, few realize that not far to the west, they can witness ancient marvels dating back centuries and millennia.

If you visit Swallow Falls State Park, it is easy to miss the last known virgin forest in Maryland. The roaring water-falls in the park and the cool waters attract more attention than walking through a forest of trees that the sun never fully illuminates.

"In the forest it is never lighter than dusk. The air, clear and clean at the 2,500-foot altitude, carries the pungent smells of pine and hemlock, the earthy odors of punkwood and leafmold," Ralph Reppert wrote in an article in *The Sun Magazine* in 1961.

The forty-acre section of white pine and eastern hemlock is estimated to be at least 330 years old and has never been cut for lumber.

"Seedlings and saplings when the Ark and the Dove sailed up the Chesapeake Bay in 1634 with Maryland's first settlers, these monarchs now have trunks up to 40 inches thick," Reppert wrote. "Their crowns may sway in the wind as high as 120 feet above the forest floor."

It has been remarked on throughout the county's history.

"Early travelers through the area told of pines with their lowest branches 100 feet from the ground," Reppert wrote.

However, as the county developed, many trees were

felled for lumber, and it looked as if this might be the fate of the trees near Swallow Falls. The size of the trees attracted the attention of lumber companies.

However, at the time, Henry Krug owned the land. He was also impressed by the size of the trees and wanted to preserve them. He resisted the offers of developers, and when he died, he deeded the property to the Masonic Grand Lodges of Pennsylvania and West Virginia.

"In 1940, shortly before lumbermen cut down a nearby stand of virgin white oak—Maryland's last—for whisky staves, the Masons sold the Swallow Falls tract to the State of Maryland," Reppert wrote.

Maintained now by the State of Maryland, the trees are allowed to live and die a natural life. On the odd occasion that a broken branch is left hanging amid other branches and poses a danger to people on the ground, it will be removed, but otherwise, the forest is left as close to untouched as possible.

Despite the measures the state has taken to preserve the forest, an estimated 2.6 acres of it might be lost if a plan to build a new bridge across the Youghiogheny River happens. The Maryland Department of Natural Resources granted an exemption to Garrett County to build a new bridge across the river on an offset to the current bridge.

Environmental groups are challenging the decision in court. Neither side denies that the some of the virgin forest will be lost.

"While the project will have an impact on the area immediately surrounding the bridge, the impacts will be limited to only those that are the minimum necessary, and the design of the bridge will allow for the removal of the central pier structure from the middle of the river," DNR Secretary Josh Kurtz wrote in a letter to Garrett County's engineering department.

He noted that the impact on the virgin hemlocks will be offset by reforestation, conservation, and mitigation practices.

In granting the county and exemption, DNR said the county must "develop, implement, and fund a 15-year Forest Conservation and Management Plan for the affected area, to include the entire limits of disturbance, in order to optimize the long-term health and sustainability of the affected old growth forest," according to an article on Yahoo News.

However, it does not mitigate the fact that a portion of the forest will be lost if the project happens.

At sixty-feet-tall, Muddy Creek Falls near this stand of trees is Maryland's highest free-falling waterfall. The source of the water for the falls is the Cranesville Pine Swamp on the border of Garrett County and Preston County, West Virginia.

The Cranesville Pine Swamp is one of the few remaining boreal bogs in the southern United States.

"Ten thousand years in the earth's geological past, this spot was formed from action of ice upon the surrounding hills," a 1961 article in *The Sun Magazine* reported.

"In the vicinity of what is now Cranesville, however, a small piece of this once vast forest remains to be what botanists call a relict colony," according to *The Glades Star*.

It survived because of the moist conditions in the high altitude, a frost pocket, and poor drainage, created an area that remained as it had been during the ice age. Scientists studied the muck in the bog and were able to identify pollen from prehistoric trees that were dated back to 7,500 B.C.

The swamp is the home of nineteen different plant communities that include sphagnum moss, speckled alder, and sedges. Round-leaved sundew and narrow-leaf gentian are found in the bog.

Black bears, porcupines, snowshoe hairs, the northern

water shrew live there. Beavers can also be found there at times. This caused a problem in the 1960s because their dams flooded sections of the swamp and the standing water killed trees and plants.

A protected trail through the prehistoric Cranesville Pine Swamp. Photo courtesy of Wikimedia Commons.

Many of these varieties of flora and fauna are rare and even endangered.

"My last trip in the Cranesville Swamp left me with the impression of a cool, mist-shrouded visit into a nether world," artist Romeo Mansueti wrote in an article in the *American Naturalist* in 1958.

The Cranesville Pine Swamp is one of three boreal bogs that were in Garrett County. Besides the Cranesville Swamp, there was one near Wolf Gap in Finzel and one near Thayerville. However, both of these were altered by mankind's encroachment and are no longer good examples of boreal bogs.

"To the casual tourist it is not particularly outstanding and many would pass it by with hardly a second glance," according to *The Glades Star*.

The people who are keenly interested in the swamp are geologists, botanists, and paleontologists.

Beginning in 1960, the Nature Conservancy began purchasing property that eventually totalled 1,600 acres. The swamp was designated the first National Natural Landmarks in the Maryland and just the eighth in U.S. in 1964. The Secretary of the Interior makes these designations after an in-depth scientific study of the proposed site. Maryland now has six such landmarks.

Garrett County's Lizzie Borden

"Lizzie Borden took an ax
And gave her mother forty whacks.
When she saw what she had done
She gave her father forty-one."

L izzie Borden allegedly killed her parents with an axe. If she did, she never faced justice for the crime. Not only was she tried and acquitted in 1893 for the murder of her father and stepmother, she went on to live the rest of her life in the house.

Garrett County has its own axe murderess who was never brought to justice for her crime and lived her life on the same property where she killed her husband.

Susan Murphy Male was married to James Wilmore Male. James was only the second generation Male. His father was a Native American who traveled with Gen. Braddock and was known to carry letters for people, which led to him being called "Mail."

"At some time during the march, either before Braddock's defeat or one the subsequent retreat over the mountains, the Indian detached himself from the command, took as his wife a negro girl who apparently was a member of the force, and settled down somewhere in what now is Garrett County," according to *The Glades Star.*

When Mail started being introduced to his neighbors, he took the given name of Wilmer. It is also around this time that Mail became his last name and morphed into Male.

The Males supposedly had four children - John, Lewis, Harriet, and Ells - although only the location of John's grave is known. Besides being a mother and wife, Susan was also worked as a midwife and herb doctor.

Susan Male. Reprinted with permission from the Garrett County Historical Society.

"One instance is recalled when she cured what was said to be a case of dropsy by the application of a piece of sod heated in the oven of the kitchen stove," according to an article in *The Glades Star*.

The family lived on a farm just south of Deep Creek Lake between Altamont and Green Glade.

On a cold winter day in 1873, James supposedly got drunk and threatened to kill Susan. Worried, Susan gathered the children and hid them in a haystack. One version of the story says that one of her sons shot at his father with a rifle and missed. Susan then found the axe used to cut firewood and snuck back into the house.

She found her husband passed out in a corner. Susan took the axe to him and cut off his head.

She supposedly went to Cumberland, which was supposed to have been the county capital at the time. However, Garrett County had formed the previous year, so either James's death date is incorrect, or Susan may have gone to Oakland.

At the county seat, Susan told the authorities what she had done, but no action was taken. *The Glades Star* also notes that the court records had been searched for a reference to the murder, but none was found.

James is buried in the Hardesty Family Cemetery on Chadderton School Road. His name stands out because he is a non-Hardesty in a family cemetery. Find-a-Grave lists only seven graves there. Five of them are Hardestys. One man was married to Hardesty, and then there is James's grave, which is also the oldest grave in the cemetery.

Susan lived another eleven years, dying in 1884 at the age of sixty-one. She is listed as being buried in Deer Park Cemetery in the county. This can only be assumed because her grave is unmarked, although it is said to be under a tamarack tree.

One version of this story says that James was living at the Green Glades Tavern when he was killed. Although the tavern was in the vicinity of the farm, there is no indication that James lived there. That's not to say he didn't visit to get drunk.

Whitewater Adventure on a Mountaintop

A bove Deep Creek Lake, high on Marsh Mountain, is some of the best whitewater rafting in the country. Mountaintops are not where you typically find rivers for rafting.

However, the mountaintop is home to Adventure Sports Center International, the world's only mountaintop recirculating whitewater course.

After the 1989 Whitewater Slalom World Championships were held on the Savage River, Sergi Orsi, president of the International Canoe Federation, encouraged organizers the event to build a pump-powered artificial whitewater course in a more accessible location nearby. This is because while the Savage River was a wonderful location for the championships, it wasn't easy to reach, especially with the number of people involved in and attending the championships.

The Wisp Ski Resort already had a pump-filled mountaintop reservoir to supply water to its snowmaking machines in the winter. It was decided to locate the waterway next to the reservoir, which created a summertime use for the reservoir.

The supporting infrastructure, such as roads, motels, and restaurants that primarily served the ski resort, also had a new summer use.

Even with the existing reservoir and infrastructure, it cost $24 million. It was the third pump-powered artificial whitewater course in North America, but it is the only mountaintop recirculating whitewater course in the world.

McLaughlin Whitewater Design Group designed the center on 550 acres. The company used a channel shaped like a natural streambed and lined with natural boulders blasted from the mountaintop. While it gives the course a somewhat natural look, the irregular surfaces dampen water surges that can happen in geometric-shaped artificial channels. The course is 1,700 feet long with twenty-four feet of vertical drop. It creates reliable whitewater that ranges from class I to class IV rapids. This allows for Olympic standard white water rafting and canoe/kayak slalom to beginner-level experiences.

The first of four spillway drops at the Adventure Sports Center International artificial whitewater course. Photo courtesy of Howard Morland on Wikimedia Commons.

"We can control a lot of the variables that you can't on a wild river and thus have a course be in one place that can accommodate both an outright beginner up to an Olympic-level canoer or kayaker," Matt Taylor told the *Cumberland Times-News.* He was the center's executive director and a two-time Olympian in Whitewater canoeing.

The center opened in May 2007. Besides whitewater and rafting training, it also offers things for the general public, such as guided raft trips, inflatable kayak rentals, and riverboard rentals.

"Spring is Whitewater season in Garrett County," said Taylor. "We take people rafting on the Whitewater course as early as the middle of April, but the bulk of our traffic occurs during the summer months, especially when the local rivers are low and it is hot outside."

The center was quickly utilized for competitions, including the 2014 World Championship slalom competition. The course needed to be modified somewhat for the championships, and the races were held September 16 to 21, 2014.

Even when not used for competitions, it was a popular place for members of the U.S. Olympic Kayak/Canoe Team to train. Not surprising, since two of the team members were Adventure Sports Center International trainers.

"This course is more realistic," team member Casey Eichfeld told the newspaper. "There is more concrete with other manmade courses."

The course continues operating today, out of sight at the top of the mountain.

Friendsville Loses Six Sons in Vietnam

W hen word that Air Force Sgt. Tommy Fike had gone missing during a mission in Vietnam on December 4, 1971, his parents in Friendsville still held out hope that he was alive.

"Maybe they've got him mixed up with somebody else," Virginia Fike told the Baltimore *Evening Sun*, "Maybe they captured him, and he's a prisoner of war."

Their hope was short-lived.

Their son, who had hoped to be home for Christmas because his enlistment was up, came home on Dec. 13 in a coffin.

He was the sixth serviceman from Friendsville to die in the Vietnam War. Four of the young men had enlisted while two had been drafted.

"That means Vietnam has claimed 1 out of every 100 Friendsville residents, a tragic statistic that no other Maryland town—and hopefully few in the United States—can claim," the *Evening Sun* reported.

The other Friendsville men killed in Vietnam were:

• Marine PFC Danny Nicklow, killed on March 16, 1967 – The enemy attacked his platoon near Quang Tri, six miles south of the demilitarized zone. Nicklow was killed in the ensuing fighting.

• Marine LCpl Ross Fike, killed on May 16, 1967 – He was killed when a truck was he riding in ran over a land mine outside of Da Nang.

- Army Spl. Wayne Hook, killed on June 17, 1967 – He was killed in a firefight shortly after being released from a Japanese hospital. He had been treated there for four months after being wounded in another action.

Wayne Hook

- Army Spl. Rodger Garlick, killed on March 17, 1969 – He died in a firefight with the enemy at Bien Hoa. He was scheduled to return home on May 28.
- Air Force Airman 1st Class Norman Eugene Thomas, killed on November 17, 1969 – Thomas died when a plane he was on crashed near Quan Loi Air Base. He had previously survived another crash.

When Tommy Fike's body returned home, it opened a lot of old wounds over all the boys that Friendsville had lost to the war.

Roger Garlick

Norman Eugene Thomas

"Maybe Friendsville should be exempt from the draft," Wayne Friend told the *Evening Sun*. Although he hadn't been drafted, he had graduated with Garlick, Ross, and Tommy Fike.

When Nicklow's father, Walt, heard the news of his son's death, the veteran of 11 years in the U.S. Navy's first impulse was to re-enlist. He hoped that by fighting, he could save someone else's son from dying.

Danny Nicklow

Garlick's father, Ralph, said of his son, "You couldn't get him to kill a rabbit or a bird. He never shot a rifle in his life until he went in the Army. He didn't believe in killing."

Some of the dead servicemen had seen the military as a way to get out of their impoverished hometown and to be able to use the G.I. Bill to afford to go to college. Their plans hadn't worked out so well, though.

With the return of Fike's body, residents had to wonder if there would be a seventh casualty. Fifteen Friendsville men were serving in the military, and five of them were serving in Vietnam.

Ross Fike

Thankfully, when the U.S. withdrew from Vietnam on March 29, 1973, all 15 of the servicemen were still alive.

In all, Western Maryland and vicinity lost 62 young men in the Vietnam War.

Tommy Fike

Indians Attack Settlers
on Snowy Creek

During the 1700s, Western Maryland was still the frontier of the United States. Settlers were pioneers who pushed westward seeking land and riches. They traversed the mountains, floated along the rivers, and looking for land.

The Native Americans in the region saw these settlers as a threat and attacked them from time to time. Small forts sprung up along the edge of the frontier. They were places where the settlers could find some level of safety.

James Brain was an English immigrant who came to America to find a better life. Brain and his wife Nancy bought 400 acres along Three Forks Creek in 1774 but only lived there a few years. The threat of an Indian attack got to them, and they moved to the safety of Friends Fort on the Youghiogheny River in 1777. They stayed there through the winter, and the following spring, they left the safety of the fort.

The Brain Family temporarily moved in with the Richard Powell Family on Snowy Creek near the West Virginia–Maryland border. Brain planned to help his friend finish repairs to his home while waiting for the Indian threat to pass. Then he would move his family back to their home on Three Forks Creek.

On April 11, 1778, five Indians approached the Brain house where Richard Powell's family was staying. Some travelers were also spending the night, which filled the cabin to capacity.

During the night, the Indians surrounded the cabin and watched it. When morning came, about a dozen males came out of the house and started competing amongst themselves, shooting at various targets.

The Indians decided that the odds against them were too great, and they left. However, the men were only a group of travelers staying together for safety. They had spent the night at the home, and after breakfast, the travelers continued on their way.

Brain, one of his sons, and two of Powell's sons left a short time after that, carrying clapboards to build a cabin that was a long walk off. The Indians heard the group walking along with their burden, and they turned back to investigate. They concealed themselves along the path and watched the group pass.

The Indians fired on the Whites, hitting Brain.

"He was then tomahawked and scalped, while another of the party followed and caught the son as he was attempting to escape by flight," according to *Chronicles of Border Warfare: A History of the Settlement by the Whites, of North-Western Virginia, and of the Indian Wars and Massacres in that section of the State.*

Two of Brain's sons and one of Powell's son were nearby. They heard the shots, but they believed it was a hunter searching for deer.

"Three Indians came running toward them, bearing their guns in one hand and their tomahawks in the other," according to *Chronicle of Border Warfare.*

One of the boys froze in place and was taken prisoner. Powell's son was caught as he tried to run. The third boy, one of Powell's sons, outran the Indians. He hid in some brush, waited until the Indians passed him, and then he ran off in the opposite direction.

"The little prisoners were then brought together, and one of Mr. Powell's sons, being discovered to have but one eye, was stripped naked, had a tomahawk sunk into his head, a spear ran through his body and the scalp then removed from his bleeding head," according to *Chronicle of Border Warfare*.

Powell's son was the boy who escaped the Indians. He fled to Ashby's Fort on Cherry Creek, eight miles away. He told the people there what had happened. A party of armed men quickly set off for the homestead.

Meanwhile, the Indians asked one of their captives, Benjamin Brain, how many men were in the house, and the boy told them twelve men were still in the house, which the Indians apparently believed having seen the travelers earlier. When the Indians asked Benjamin how far away the nearest fort was, the boy told them two miles. He did this, knowing there were no men in the house and Ashby's Fort was eight miles away on Cherry Creek.

"His object was to save his mother and the other women and children from captivity or death, by inducing them to believe that it would be extremely dangerous to venture near the house," according to *Chronicle of Border Warfare*.

Deciding not to press their luck, the Indians left, taking Benjamin and Isaac Brain with them. When the men from Ashby's Fort arrived, the Indians were gone.

They had been so stealthy that Nancy Brain didn't realize that her husband was dead until the men from the fort arrived.

Benjamin was held captive six years before he escaped. Isaac Brain was never heard of or seen again.

Garrett's First and Only Hanging

I
n 1883, ten and a half years after Garrett County formed, the county had its first murder. By the end of the year, it had its first and only hanging.

John Herbert Smith was a former slave who had worked a variety of jobs before taking a position as a construction foreman for the Baltimore and Ohio Railroad. He lived near Gorman and was said to be a good worker.

He was also an acquaintance, some said, a friend, of Josiah Harden, a Confederate Army veteran who worked as a shoemaker. His wife, Harriet, and two of their five children lived near Gorman. Harden had had some legal problems in the past because he had forged a check, but he wasn't considered vicious.

Although Harden denied being friends with Smith, the latter visited the Hardens frequently. "Later, many people believed that Mrs. Harden and her mother had encouraged Smith's visits," Wayne Wilt wrote for *The Glades Star.*

The *Baltimore Sun* pointed out that it may have been Harriet whom Smith "was on good terms with the Harding [sic] family; so much so that Harding is said to have quarreled with his wife about it."

One evening in May 1883, Smith showed up at the Harden's home around 7 p.m. "He paid Harden five cents for repairing his boots, and while there, he made a statement to Harden's son, Robert, 'Your father don't like me very much,'" Wilt wrote.

He said he had a present for each member of the family,

and he would have to return with them. He asked Harden for a drink of whiskey. Harden refused, saying it was his bedtime. Smith told him to go to bed, but Harden didn't want to do it with Smith still in the house.

He left around 8 p.m. "He continued to promise gifts, stating that he had a nice instrument in his pocket, which makes nice music, but he would not have as much fun as he expected since the Harden relatives were away," Wilt wrote.

Smith apparently went somewhere where he could get a drink of whiskey. Witnesses at a saloon heard him threaten Harden. He didn't say why he was angry with a man who was supposed to be a friend, but he went out looking for him.

After Smith had left, the Harden family settled down for the evening. Harden's 9-year-old daughter was sitting next to her father with their backs to a window. Robert Harden, Josiah and Harriet's son, was sitting near his mother on the other side of the room.

About half an hour after Smith left, two shots were fired through the window.

Harden jumped up, holding his shoulder. "Don't do that Smith. Don't do that anymore. That's enough of that," he yelled.

Harden told his family to run upstairs while he went to the door to confront Smith. Smith smashed in the door and fired three more shots at Harden, hitting him in the back and neck.

As Harden fell to the floor, mortally wounded, Smith ran upstairs. He grabbed Harriet, forced her into the nearby woods, and raped her.

Robert ran out to try to help his mother, but Smith hit him on the head with the butt of his gun. Then he pointed it at the boy. Robert ran back into the house.

By the time Harriet returned, Harden was dead. She and

her children went to a neighbor's house to report the crime. Garrett County had its first murder victim.

Smith goes to the gallows

In 1883, John Herbert Smith shot and killed Josiah Harden. It was a cold-blooded murder of a man with whom Smith was said to be friendly. To make matters worse, Smith raped Harriet Harden right after he killed her husband.

After Harriet reported the crime, the police went to Smith's house and ordered him to surrender. He told them the police he was coming out. Time passed, and when Smith still hadn't come out, the police entered the house.

Smith wasn't inside.

He had climbed up the chimney and gotten away.

Authorities started a manhunt for the accused murderer and rapist. Meanwhile, a coroner's jury convened to examine Harden's body and other evidence. They found Smith responsible for Harden's death.

Days after the murder, Garrett County authorities discovered a man had been arrested in Winchester who matched Smith's description, although the man said his last name was Jackson. State's Attorney John Veitch sent Jeremiah Browning to Winchester to see if the prisoner was Smith. Browning confirmed it was Smith and arrangements were made to extradite Smith back to Oakland.

Smith's trial began on Sept. 18 and lasted three days. Witnesses testified Smith had been angry with Harden, whom he said cheated him on a business transaction. Another witness said Smith admitted to killing Harden and said his only regret was that he hadn't killed Harriet.

Smith professed his innocence, saying he had heard the shots from the house, heard the children crying, and saw two men running away from the house.

Not only was it a weak defense, but witnesses also testified "Smith was trying to encourage other black people in the community to lie and say they were at his house on the night of the murder playing cards and dancing, but they refused to lie for him," according to *The Glades Star*.

Smith apparently had also wanted them to rally behind him and attack the law enforcement officers when they had come to arrest him.

The jury deliberated just a half hour before finding Smith guilty of murder. Judge Alvey sentenced Smith to hang.

Smith argued he hadn't received justice, and he wanted a new trial. He said if he had been guilty, he would have confessed it and not gone through with the trial. He also said some witnesses who could have supported him were poor and couldn't take off work for the trial or they would have lost their jobs.

As deputies removed him from the courthouse, Smith said, "You may hang the body, but you can't hang the soul. You will be judged yourself someday."

On Oct. 4, Smith complained he was ill. When jailer James Cropp entered the cell, Smith attacked him with a bucket. Cropp stabbed Smith before he escaped. Smith found a hatchet and used it to break his leg shackles. However, his wound proved too painful, and he surrendered himself the next morning.

In preparation for the hanging, gallows were built. "The jail yard has been inclosed [sic] by a twenty-feet high board fence, the rear doors of the jail building opening into the yard, so that the prisoner can be brought from his cell into the year and thence to the scaffold without being seen from the outside," the *Baltimore Sun* reported.

The night before the execution, Rev. Benjamin Ison visited with Smith, who still proclaimed his innocence. However, when Ison visited again in the morning, Smith finally admitted his guilt. "He said he had nothing against Harden, but blamed liquor for the killing, and he had been encouraged to do it," according to *The Glades Star.*

The woman Smith had been living with also visited with her two children, one of which was also Smith's. He kissed his child through the bars of the cell before they left.

Smith asked for a shave and a clean shirt. He said that if he was "going to be murdered, he wanted to die in style," according to the *National Republican.*

He ate his last meal and smoked a cigar. He was still smoking the cigar as he was led to the gallows.

On the scaffold below the gallows, Smith said, "Farewell to everybody. God bless you all. It's very hard when a man comes to die like this, but it's no difference what the death is, so the soul is ready to live with God. I am ready to die. I weep, not because I am to die, but because of the deed for which I am accused. I don't deny it. I done it. I, John Herbert Smith. But, I was persuaded to do it, and under the influence of liquor at the time. I have prayed to God to forgive me and hope my fellow men have forgiven me."

He then turned to the sheriff and said he was ready. A black bag was placed over his head, and the body fell at 1:14 p.m. on Nov. 16. Twenty people were in the courtyard to witness the first and last hanging in the county.

Snow and More Snow

T he call came in that Thomas J. Johnson needed an ambulance. He was seriously ill and needed to get to the hospital. Normally, it wouldn't be a problem, but in early 1958, getting anywhere in Garrett County was, to say the least, difficult.

The ambulance attempted to reach him, but it couldn't get through to Johnson's Herrington Manor home. Help came in the form of bulldozers and snow plows that struggled to carve a path through drifting snow as high as fifteen feet. It took six hours for the plows to reach the sixty-seven-year-old Johnson and rush him to Garrett Memorial Hospital.

During another incident that winter, Trooper First Class Robert Henline walked three miles through deep snow that vehicles couldn't get through to deliver medicine to a desperate family near Gorman.

Other incidents occurred, some serious and some just major inconveniences, but there were a lot of them. In seven weeks in 1958, nearly 112 inches of snow fell on the county, beating out the previously bad winter of 1936. No other winter in the twentieth century to that point even came close.

The *Cumberland Sunday Times* reported that the bad weather "practically isolated most of the county despite heroic efforts of State Roads and county roads crews, National Guardsmen and other volunteers."

Although the first snows of the new year had fallen mid-January, the first big storm came at the end of the month. Ten inches of snow fell on January 24, followed by three more inches two days later. "For a short time on Friday afternoon there was snow, sleet and ice falling at the same time," *The Republican* reported. A heavy fog also slowed things down.

The heavy snows led to the rare occurrence of closing Garrett County schools in the county for three days at the beginning of February.

A picture of how high up snow can get piled during the winter in Garrett County. Reprinted with permission from the Garrett County Historical Society.

"It was the first time in several years that there had been the loss of even one day of school," *The Republican* noted.

School Superintendent Willard Hawkins said he "was

afraid to put the buses on the roads because of poor visibility and icy conditions." *The Republican* reported that Hawkins had intended to resume school on the third days until he found out that many children and teachers were still snowbound.

A week later, nearly ten inches of snow fell on three consecutive days. Pleasant Valley, Kempton, North Glade, Sanders Lane, and Herrington Manor were the worst hit, reporting snow drifts of fifteen feet or more. With visibility near zero, the Maryland State Police issued an emergency travel only order.

The blizzard left about forty percent of the county roads impassable for two days, according to Paul DeWitt, assistant county engineer. Garrett County had 140 men working forty-five snow plows around the clock to try to open and clear the 740 miles of county roads.

State road crews were running twenty snow plows and a giant snow-blower over the 158 miles of state roads in the county. The only state road that was impassable was Route 495, between Bittinger and Grantsville.

With so much snow on the ground, the snow plows were only able to push it so far off the road before running into previous piles of snow that had been pushed off the road. "By that time there was no place to push it and consequently many of the highways drifted completely over," *The Republican* reported.

In Oakland, snow and vehicles competed for space and the snow often won. "Parking space was at a premium and many of those who found places at the edges of the drifts found themselves unable to move when they returned to their cars," *The Republican* noted.

All the snow busted the county's budget that year with rented equipment costing $1,000 a day and snow removal equipment using 2,000 gallons of gasoline a day.

Although the snow totals blew away previous snowfall records in the county, at least the temperature records still stood. In 1958, the temperature fell to -17 degrees, but the 1912 record was -40 degrees.

Moonshining in the Mountains

W hen the sale, production and transportation of alcohol were banned in the United States in 1920, Western Marylanders had to choose between becoming teetotalers or criminals. Many law-abiding citizens chose the latter.

Bootlegging in Garrett County was going on before Prohibition, as it was many other places. The difference was Prohibition made it more profitable and attractive to people.

An early story about a bootlegger appeared in the Oakland Republican in 1915. A man sent word ahead that he would be driving a wagon loaded with nitroglycerin from Oakland to Grafton, West Virginia.

"Passing teams of horses and farmers stood with bated breath as the outfit passed with its 'dare-devil' driver bouncing about on the seat, whipping up the horses and thundering over rocks," the *Oakland Republican* reported.

However, this man was actually hauling 200 gallons of illegal liquor. He traveled to the Wendel coal mines a few miles from Grafton.

He quickly sold the liquor and then he even auctioned off his wagon and team for an additional $200.

"It is said the receipts from the entire sale were sufficient to maintain the bootlegger in comfort the remainder of his life," according to the Republican.

Unpopular law

Though Prohibition was not popular nationwide, Maryland was nearly defiant in its attitude toward the law. Maryland was the only state not to pass an enforcement act, and it still called itself a "wet", not "dry", state.

A *Cumberland Evening Times* editorial proclaimed in 1920, "On the bootlegging proposition the police commissioner is probably right in his conclusion that the United States army would not be able to stop drunkenness entirely. This probably would be true so long us preventing drunkenness depends upon the enforcement of so extreme and unreasonable a measure as the Volstead act which, in its entirety is not respected by one reasonable person in ten."

Police found moonshine in a vehicle after it crashed. Photo courtesy of the Library of Congress.

However, no matter how unpopular Prohibition was, law enforcement officials did their jobs. According to Herman Miller in *Cumberland, Maryland, thought the Eyes of Herman J. Miller*, so many arrests were made for bootlegging and illegal liquor sales during Prohibition that the Allegany County Jail couldn't hold everyone at times, and the excess prisoners had to be kept in the Garrett County Jail in Oakland.

Besides Allegany County's overflow, Garrett County had its own prisoners to deal with as well. Bootleggers regularly appeared in *The Republican* as they were sentenced to prison time.

George Hawkins

One of the reasons for so many bootlegger arrests in Western Maryland was due to the work of federal agent William Hawkins. He could be considered Garrett County's Eliot Ness.

"He could not be bribed, and he achieved quite a local reputation for his persistence in tracking down illicit whiskey. At one point, he trailed a bootlegger through the snow for several miles, from the swamp where the man confiscated a cache of moonshine," Harry Stegmaier wrote in *Allegany County-A History.*

"Hundreds of stills were captured and dismantled by him, and at no time was he known to show favor to the 'influential citizens' known to be bootleggers. His friends say this impartial and honest activity indirectly brought his dismissal," *The Republican* reported.

His record of success made him enemies. In trying to get him fired or transferred, they charged him with misconduct, but the investigations always found him to be innocent.

He became such a thorn in the sides of bootleggers lost his job as a federal enforcement officer in May 1924. "Hawkins attributed his dismissal to pressure brought to bear by local politicians and others; who, while appearing to work for prohibition and law enforcement, were actually in league with a bootlegging combine," *The Republican* reported.

Despite the comparisons, Western Maryland actually had very little problem with organized crime, such as what was seen in Chicago during Prohibition. The reason for this is that nearly all the moonshine in Mountain Maryland was made locally, so organized crime never had much of an opportunity to get its foot in the door here.

Police in Tennessee pose with a load of moonshine they confiscated during Prohibition. Photo courtesy of the Library of Congress.

Hiding the stills

Because manufacturing liquor was illegal, the stills needed to be hidden out of sight of law-enforcement officials. Old mines and remote areas in the mountains were popular locations to hill stills.

If someone stumbled upon one of them, they needed to be cautious and lucky. John R. Paige wrote in "Holy Cross

Camp of Deer Park, Maryland, The Foundation Years: 1930-1945" tells the story of a group of seminarians with the Congregation of the Holy Cross who were driving through the mountains when their Model T truck broke down. They discovered that their Army/Navy surplus khaki clothes made them look like revenue agents.

"Some gunmen came out of the woods and asked us who we were and what we were doing. I explained and they opened up the truck to examine the contents, see what we had. Because we had khaki clothes on, they were suspicious of us. After we had satisfied their curiosity they insisted we take a drink, moonshine. We refused for our stomach's sake and then they wanted to give us money. We took it because it would be wise to take it and not irritate them. They let us go then. Later on, we heard that another party had blundered into their camp and were killed," one of the priests told Paige.

At one "moonshine plant," agents discovered in 1925 in the mountains near Jennings, "The smoke from the wood fire heating the still was conducted by a pipe up a hollow chestnut tree on the hillside above the scene of operations, forty feet in the air. The still itself was hidden in a rocky arcade in a deep glen in the woods and concealed from all sides. Entrance was gained by going up on a precipice and dropping down by a stairway out on the hillside," *The Republican* reported.

The 100-gallon still had been constructed from new copper. Water was supplied from a spring 200 yards away. Everything used in the operation was clean and scrubbed. Even the mash vats (and the agents found fifteen barrels) were covered with screens to keep out flies, insects, and vermin.

It was an operation put together to create high-quality moonshine. The agents said that the moonshine didn't have the yeasty smell that a lot of moonshine had.

It shouldn't be too surprising because one of the moon-shiners was George Burkholder, who many considered the "king of the Garrett County bootleggers." It was said he was often referred to as "King George."

A dismantled still that federal agents confiscated. Photo courtesy of the Library of Congress.

Burkholder had served time in the Maryland Penitentiary. After he was released, he became a coal miner for a while and then a Pentecostal preacher. However, once the Volstead Act was passed, he found his calling as a moonshiner.

He started in West Virginia, but the federal agents made it too difficult for him to maintain his business, so he moved into Garrett County.

"It appears that he so managed the business that he reaped about all the profits and the other fellows always fell into the hands of the prohibition officers when they periodically visited that section of the county," *The Republican* reported.

He was so successful that he bought himself a new touring car that he drove around the county in. He also bought a truck to use for delivering his moonshine.

The federal agents who raided his still also confiscated his car, which he left behind when fled the scene of the raid. He was so confident of his power in the county that he showed up in Oakland to have the federal agents arrested for stealing his car. Instead, the authorities there arrested him.

Trying to avoid jail

Bootleggers could be just as creative in trying to stay out of jail as they were in hiding their stills. Some forged checks to post bail for friends.

One bootlegger, "Western Bill" Harvey, was caught at a seventy-five gallon still operating the pump attached to the pressure tank of a gasoline burner when federal agents arrived.

When brought before the judge, he said, "I lost the pump from my car, and I thought that if I took a walk through the woods I'd find some of those bootleggers using it on their still. And I was right, too. I did find the pump just where I expected."

"Then you knew of the still?" asked the agent questioning him.

"Oh, no! I just discovered it when looking for my pump," Harvey said.

Another bootlegger, Thomas Johnson, tried to get his powerful friend to get him off on charges.

"Distinguished lineage was invoked in a plea for clemency by former State Senator William A. Gunter, who said Johnson was a great-grandson of Thomas Johnson, first Governor of Maryland. Johnson had pled guilty to bootlegging in

Garrett county. Mr. Gunter declared Johnson was not a 'common' bootlegger, but the scion of a noble house who had made a mistake," *The Republican* reported.

Taking advantage

While most bootleggers actually made moonshine to sell, some simply took advantage of people's desires for illegal booze. *The Republican* discovered something interesting about neighboring Fairmont, West Virginia. "The people of Fairmont say West Virginia is really dry. The bootleggers have gone to selling coffee. If you don't believe it, ask the Java topers who contributed $200 to a former member of the 'John Barleycorn' fraternity, who unloaded 200 pints of coffee at one dollar per, at Clarksburg Monday evening."

The following morning, it became apparent that the coffee had an extra kick. "They walked the streets with their tongues lagging out—and, yes, they had a dark brown taste in their mouth's, — (that's the color of coffee, you know), and their eyes were green—not from the effects of Barleycorn, but madness."

An Oakland bootlegger had sent a message to Clarksburg saying he was coming to their town. Anyone who wanted could quench their thirst with his product for a dollar a pint. Everyone considered this a bargain because their local bootleggers were charging $1.50 a pint for moonshine.

The train from Oakland arrived, and the bootlegger was met with a crowd wanting to get a pint or two. "He stepped from the train, smiling, and after he had unloaded his luggage, he cautioned his customers not to unwrap the bottles until he had again boarded the train, for fear that the sleuths might arrest him," the newspaper reported.

He sold his 200 pints in five minutes and left on the next train with $200

The crowd quickly dispersed, with people hurrying off to sample their purchases. It turns out the bootlegger had sold the crowd coffee, and weak coffee at that. Each bottle contained just enough coffee so that it didn't taste like water.

It was estimated that the bootlegger made $198 since the coffee cost no more than $2.

The front page of *The Oakland Republican* after Prohibition was ended. It was given the same prominence as an announcement of highway projects. Photo courtesy of the author's collection.

The end of Prohibition

Due to its unpopularity, Prohibition soon ended after the election of Franklin D. Roosevelt in 1932. Even after the Volstead Act was repealed and Prohibition ended, Garrett County voted to remain a dry county in 1933. Voters even voted in a beer ban for the county. When that didn't bring work, the county tried to get their piece of the pie and proposed a two-cent-tax on bottle caps, saying it would generate

$30,000 and allow them to lower taxes. Not only was revenue estimate far overestimated, one reader wrote the Republican pointing out another flaw. "Will the bootlegger and the law breaker use county tax caps for bottles which are drunk at the bar and the table? We know very well that such will not be the case."

Moonshine made easy

Besides making moonshine (illegal liquor), bootleggers were also known to make "home brew", illegal beer, during Prohibition. Garrett County miner, Kenny Bray, wrote about some of the recipes in his unpublished memoirs.

Home brew

Ingredients: 1 can malt 0.75, 5 lb. sugar, 1 yeast cake 0.05, 5 gal. water.

Dissolve the sugar and malt in warm water. Add yeast and cover with cloth. "When it begins to ferment, a foam will form on top," Bray wrote. The foam will eventually diminish.

"To tell when it is done, you hold a lighted match down next to the surface of the liquid. If the match goes out, it is not ready. If the match continues to burn, it is ready to bottle," according to Bray.

Moonshine

Ingredients: 1 bushel corn or grain, 50 lb. sugar, 2 yeast cakes, 35-50 gal. water

Moonshine was made in stills. The two major parts of a still were the boiler and the cooling tube. Half-inch copper tubing was run from the boiler (where it was sealed with flour paste to keep an airtight seal) to the cooling tube where it coiled as it ran through the cooling tub until it reached the bottom of the tub.

The ingredients are mixed to make corn mash, which is heated in the boiler. Some bootleggers might add honey to the ingredients and let it ferment with the water and yeast. The resulting alcohol from this was called "Honey Brandy."

"When you were no longer getting alcohol from the worm, you would catch about a teaspoon from it, throw it on the fire. If it flashed, you kept cooking. If it sizzled, you stopped," Bray wrote.

The finished alcohol could be aged in charcoal to give it an amber color or vanilla extract might be added to give it an aged appearance.

The quality of the finished product was determined by shaking the bottle. The shaking caused a "bead" or chain of bubbles to form around the edge of the bottle at the top of the liquid. The longer the alcohol held the bead, the better it was considered.

The Region's Worst Tornado Hits

O n Friday afternoon, June 23, 1944, Garrett County residents noticed the sky grow grayer and the wind increase. John Keenan of Deer Park said it looked like a "fast moving mass of rolling blue clouds" while another person said it looked like two cloud masses hitting head on.

When they did, a tornado formed that wreaked havoc over five counties. This was after having ripped through parts of northern West Virginia and southwestern Pennsylvania a short time earlier. People ran for their cellars as the winds increased over 200 miles per hour. The tornado twisted along the terrain, moving back and forth over miles "damaging scores of homes, uprooting trees, telegraph and telephone poles and destroying gardens and blocking highways," according to the *Cumberland Evening Times*.

The newspaper called it the worst weather catastrophe ever to hit this area. "The angry wind cut a clean path for miles, knocking down, destroying or carrying away homes, barns, churches, school buildings, stores and railroad stations," the newspaper reported. The Baltimore and Ohio Railroad was closed for two hours between Oakland and Altamont.

Clarence Mimna of Deer Park sent his four children into the cellar of their home. He was about to join them when the winds collapsed the house. It took him hours to get his children free of the wreckage.

People found furniture a quarter mile away from their

homes. Cars were tossed up to 500 yards away from where they had been parked.

Besides Garrett, the tornado also hit Grant, Tucker, Barbour, and Randolph counties in West Virginia. However, it was part of a larger weather system that created tornadoes in Maryland, Pennsylvania, and West Virginia. Particularly hard hit was Shinnston in Harrison County, West Virginia. The town was virtually destroyed when an F4 tornado (Fujita scale) with winds between 207 and 260 mph hit it.

A family scours through the wreckage of their home after tornadoes swept through Maryland, Pennsylvania, and West Virginia in 1944. Photo courtesy of Wikimedia Commons.

Abrams Creek, West Virginia, south of Garrett County, saw a tornado cut across U.S. 50, leaving a swath 100 yards wide as it tore homes apart. However, "Between Abrams Creek and Red House in Maryland, there was little evidence of the storm except in places where a few limbs were torn from trees," according to the *Cumberland Sunday Times*.

The initial count put eighteen people killed locally and 250 injured. This included three people from Garrett County who were killed: Mr. and Mrs. James Sebold and six-year-old Robert Paugh, who all died when their homes collapsed on them. Another forty Garrett Countians were injured. When the number of victims overwhelmed the beds available in hospitals in the affected areas, victims were transported to five other hospitals, including Allegany Hospital and Cumberland Memorial Hospital. Tucker County Hospital, Potomac Valley Hospital, and Elkins City Hospital also received victims.

More than 100 homes were destroyed or left uninhabitable, leaving more than 500 people homeless. In Thomas, West Virginia, alone, twenty-five homes were destroyed and twenty-five damaged.

Sgt. Charles Magaha of the Maryland State Police surveyed the county and said the devastation of the Sand Flat area southwest of Deep Creek Lake was the worst he had ever seen. He reported seeing farm animals with their heads turned 180 degrees and other that were "blown inside out." He said was looked at a twenty-acre field of corn that looked like nothing more than a field of dirt.

The three-state tornado outbreak left 170 people dead, and it remains the worst tornado ever to hit West Virginia.

Moonshine Can Kill
One Way or Another

I n early 1931, a middle-aged woman walked into the Sturgiss Pharmacy in Oakland. She introduced herself as Rosa McRobie and asked for a dram of strychnine. When the pharmacist asked why she needed so much poison, Rosa said her husband had asked her to get some "to kill rats and squirrels," according to the *Oakland Republican*.

A few days later, Dr. E. E. Sollars responded to an emergency call at the home of Mike Felda and his wife. He went into the house and found Mike dead, his eyes dilated and "his mouth and throat in such condition that he doubted if moonshine liquor alone could have killed him," the *Cumberland Evening Times* reported.

Not everyone was so confident the liquor didn't kill him. Moonshine, depending on its formulas, could be deadly. Bootleggers sometimes mixed in other things like iodine and tobacco juice so that their moonshine would look or taste a certain way. Batches could also contain methyl alcohol because they hadn't been distilled enough to remove the harmful chemical.

Since the cause of death was not apparent, and body's appearance bothered the doctor, an autopsy was conducted. A chemist tested the viscera in Felda's body. "An autopsy performed on the dead man disclosed a quantity of poison in the stomach and more of the same kind was located in one of two bottles of liquor found in the home," the *Frederick*

News reported.

The liquor showed enough strychnine to kill six men. The coroner's jury determined Felda had been murdered.

The investigation also discovered that Felda's wife, Rosa, had used her maiden name to purchase strychnine from the pharmacy. Rosa's friend, Carrie Harvey, was the wife of a well-known Garrett County bootlegger named "Western Bill" Harvey. She had provided Rosa with two bottles of moonshine.

Police arrested Rosa and Carrie and charged them with murder.

"The women are believed to have been actuated by jealousy on the part of the wife, as it was said that she had accused her husband of infidelity," the *Cumberland Evening Times* reported. It was also pointed out that she couldn't have killed him for money because they had no life insurance.

The case went to court in Allegany County in front of Judge D. Lindley Sloan. Garrett County State's Attorney Walter W. Dawson made the case that Carrie had provided the liquor, Rosa had poisoned it, and then placed it where her husband would find it. He also told the jury that a witness heard Felda say that days before his death, he thought his wife was trying to kill him.

Rosa testified she had bought the poison to use on herself. She wanted to commit suicide because of her husband's unfaithfulness. She admitted pouring some of the poison into a bottle of liquor and throwing the rest of it away. Rosa said she put the bottle in the pocket of her dead brother's coat and tucked it away in the closet. Her husband must have found it and drank part of it.

The jury was sequestered in the Algonquin overnight. They returned with their verdict the next day at noon. Carrie was found not guilty, and the case was dropped. However, the jury found Rosa guilty of manslaughter. She was sentenced to five years in prison.

This verdict started Rosa's family wondering if this instance might not have been the first time that Rosa poisoned someone. *The Cumberland Evening Times* reported that her brother and sister had died under "peculiar circumstances."

Her brother, F. Luther McRobie, had been found dead in his bed 18 months earlier. "The coroner's jury deemed the death due to acute alcoholism, the cause ascribed to her husband's death by Mrs. Felda," according to the newspaper.

Her sister had died on a train between New York and Philadelphia. "She was thought to have been a drug addict and to have taken an overdose of drugs," according to the newspaper.

However, no investigation was ever made into their suspicions.

Centenarians for the Centennial

G arrett County was founded on November 4, 1872, and created from Allegany County the following year. During the county's founding year, several Garrett Countians were either born or infants. They grew up with the county, particularly the people who were born in 1872.

When those people were turned fifty years old, so did Garrett County, and they shared in the celebration of that milestone year. However, as their centennial birthday approached, many of those Garrett Countians passed away.

During January 1972, the Garrett County Commissioners formed a Centennial Commission of ten people. Their job was to coordinate the efforts of the county government and the Garrett County Historical Society in celebrating the 100th anniversary of the formation of Garrett County. The *Cumberland News* noted that the anniversary celebrated the act of the Maryland Legislature, giving people the right to vote on whether they wanted to form a new county "the line being drawn on the top of Big Savage Mountain to assure the necessary 10,000 population."

The vote passed, and Garrett County was formed in 1873 from Allegany County. To date, it is the last Maryland county to be formed, and it is the third-least populated county in the state.

Some planning for the centennial celebration was delayed by record-breaking February snows in the county that kept groups from meeting, but the historical society, headed by B.

JAMES RADA, JR.

O. Aiken, was soon at work planning events when the roads were open.

"Now the clock will roll back 100 years, and the farming communities and towns of the county will again hear the rumble of wagon wheels as the Appalachian Wagon Train rolls though the western corner of the state on June 20 to kick off the centennial celebration," the *Cumberland News* noted.

A float symbolizing Garrett County's pioneer heritage in the Garrett County Centennial Festival Parade. Reprinted with permission from the Garrett County Historical Society.

The wagon train consisted of fifty covered wagons drawn by oxen, horses, and mules. It left Fort Necessity in Pennsylvania on June 19 and traveled through Markleysburg, Pennsylvania; Friendsville; McHenry; Springs, Pennsylvania; and Cumberland. When the wagon train arrived at the Garrett County Fairgrounds in McHenry, it was greeted with a welcoming parade.

Other events in 1972 included a special dinner in late June and special exhibits at the historical society, Garrett Community College, and Garrett County Fair. The Autumn Glory Festival that year also celebrated the county's centennial birthday.

During the year, the American Association of Retired Persons, Chapter 770, in Garrett County sought residents who shared a birth year with the county. Three residents were found.

Jonas Broadwater was born on Oct. 10, 1871. He was a lifelong resident of the Savage River Valley who lived near Bloomington. He lived in the family homestead for most of his life. The *Cumberland News* noted that he loved telling stories of how good a shot he used to be. He and his wife Edith had raised a family of seven children.

"The Broadwater Chapel of the Dunkard Brethren Church, along the Savage River, is a monument to his religious faith, and has had an active congregation since Mr. Broadwater constructed it in 1911," according to the *Cumberland News*.

Mary Katherine Pifer was born on February 2, 1872. Although she was born in Parsons, West Virginia, she had lived most of her life in the county. She married Emery Elliott, and the couple raised four children together. Emery died in 1956.

Virginia Buncutter was born March 2, 1872. Born in Logan County, West Virginia, her family moved to Gortner when Virginia was eight. She married George Williams Sanders, and they raised six children. George died in 1915.

The AARP also arranged for President Richard Nixon to

send them birthday cards on their respective birthdays.

Sadly, no one remains who shared in Garrett County's birth year as the county moves toward its 150th birthday next year.

Acknowledgements

I wanted to thank all of those people who helped me put the *Secrets of Deep Creek Lake* together. The longer I work as a writer, the more I realize that while one person may publish a book, the effort is much richer when others assist.

I've been writing articles about the history of this region for nearly two decades. I've been doing the Secrets books for seven years. *Secrets of Garrett County* was the first book in the series. I wrote it way back in 2017, and I have a list of topics for future Secrets books that I will never be able to complete.

One great local resource for finding the stories in this book was digitized editions of *The Oakland Republican* found on the Library of Congress website. The Garrett County Historical Society (garrettcountymuseums.com) and the Ruth Enlow Library (www.relib.net) were also great resources of information I consulted. Of course, whenever I write about Western Maryland, I also check out topics and information at the Western Maryland's Historical Library (www.whilbr.org) website. Cheryl Shafer with the Deep Creek Lake Sailing Association was also generous sharing some of her lake photos with me.

Finally, I'd like to thank Grace Eyler with E Plus in Emmitsburg, Md., for not only creating another great-looking cover but also being able to create the template for the Secrets series.

I have probably missed someone who I'll remember after this book goes to print. If so, it's not because I didn't appreciate your input. I sometimes get confused juggling all of the projects that I do. If I did leave you out, mention it to me.

Meanwhile, I'm off to work on my next project.

James Rada, Jr.
March 1, 2024

About the Author

J ames Rada, Jr. is an Amazon.com bestselling author of historical fiction and non-fiction history. They include the popular books *Strike the Fuse, Canawlers,* and *Battlefield Angels: The Daughters of Charity Work as Civil War Nurses.*

He lives in Gettysburg, Pa., where he works as a freelance writer. James has received numerous awards from the Maryland-Delaware-DC Press Association, Associated Press, Maryland State Teachers Association, Society of Professional Journalists, and Community Newspapers Holdings, Inc. for his newspaper writing.

If you would like to be kept up to date on new books being published by James or ask him questions, he can be reached by e-mail at *jimrada@yahoo.com.*

To see James' other books or to order copies on-line, go to *www.jamesrada.com.*

PLEASE LEAVE A REVIEW

If you enjoyed this book, please help other readers find it. Reviews help authors get more exposure for their books. Please take a few minutes to review this book at *Amazon.com* or *Goodreads.com*. Thank you, and if you sign up for his mailing list at *jamesrada.com*, you can get FREE ebooks.

WANT TO KNOW MORE SECRETS?

Find out the little-known stories and hidden history of Maryland and Pennsylvania with the Secrets series from James Rada, Jr.

Available wherever books are sold.

www.ingramcontent.com/pod-product-compliance
Lightning Source LLC
Chambersburg PA
CBHW060513130626
46553CB00002B/477